Colin Bamford

Cambridge International AS and A Level

Economics

Workbook

CAMBRIDGE
UNIVERSITY PRESS

University Printing House, Cambridge CB2 8BS, United Kingdom

One Liberty Plaza, 20th Floor, New York, NY 10006, USA

477 Williamstown Road, Port Melbourne, VIC 3207, Australia

314–321, 3rd Floor, Plot 3, Splendor Forum, Jasola District Centre, New Delhi – 110025, India

79 Anson Road, 06–04/06, Singapore 079906

Cambridge University Press is part of the University of Cambridge.

It furthers the University's mission by disseminating knowledge in the pursuit of education, learning and research at the highest international levels of excellence.

www.cambridge.org
Information on this title: education.cambridge.org/9781108401586

First published 2018

20 19 18 17 16 15 14 13 12 11 10 9 8 7 6 5 4

Printed in Poland by Opolgraf

A catalogue record for this publication is available from the British Library

ISBN 978-1-108-40158-6 Paperback

Additional resources for this publication at cambridge.org/9781108401586

Cambridge University Press has no responsibility for the persistence or accuracy of URLs for external or third-party internet websites referred to in this publication, and does not guarantee that any content on such websites is, or will remain, accurate or appropriate. Information regarding prices, travel timetables, and other factual information given in this work is correct at the time of first printing but Cambridge University Press does not guarantee the accuracy of such information thereafter.

Past paper examination questions throughout are reproduced by permissions of Cambridge Assessment International Education.

Cambridge Assessment International Education bears no responsibility for the example answers to questions taken from its past paper questions which are contained in this publication.

All exam-style questions and sample answers in this title were written by the authors. In examinations, the way marks are awarded may be different.

....

Contents

iii

Acknowledgements

I would like to thank Claire Handy for her editorial advice and Cathryn Freear of CUP for guiding me through the production process. My thanks are also due to Diane Bramley for her assistance with word processing and to my daughter Emily for the original idea for the artwork on page 1. Finally, and by no means least, I hope that this workbook and the corresponding answers will not only help students and teachers develop their knowledge of Economics but also raise awareness of how important a study of Economics is in fostering a better understanding of the global village in which we all work and live.

Colin Bamford, 2017

The authors and publishers acknowledge the following sources of copyright material and are grateful for the permissions granted. While every effort has been made, it has not always been possible to identify the sources of all the material used, or to trace all copyright holders. If any omissions are brought to our notice, we will be happy to include the appropriate acknowledgements on reprinting

Past examination questions throughout are reproduced by permission of Cambridge Assessment International Education.

Image in Developing Skills chapter adapted from an original drawing by Emily Bamford; Figure 0.2 adapted from article in the Daily Sabah, October 8, 2014; Table 0.3, 0.4, 0.5 adapted from Table 1.2 pages 13, 57, BRICS Joint Statistical Publication 2015; Figure 0.3 adapted from 'Gross domestic product (GDP) of the BRIC countries from 2010 to 2020 (in billion U.S. dollars)' © Statista 2017; Figure 1.2 adapted from 'The NHS budget and how it has changed'. Source: Department of Health annual report and accounts 2015/16; Central government supply estimates 2016-17, supplementary estimates and new estimates – Feb 2017; HM Treasury GDP deflators at market prices, and money GDP March 2017 (Quarterly national accounts, March 2017) © The Kings Fund http://www.kingsfund.org.uk; Ch2 Data response adapted from article 'Cocoa crop hit by worst Saharan storm in two decades' by Isis Almeida © Bloomberg Business Newspaper 19 January 2016; Figure 4.1 adapted from 'The changes in consumer prices and the purchasing power of the Namibian dollar from 2003 to 2013' © Namibian Statistics Agency 2014; Figure 4.2 adapted from 'US Dollar to Brazilian Real Exchange Rate Chart from 2012 to 2016' © Ycharts Inc; Figure 4.3 adapted from 'Current account and goods trade balance, 2010-2016, Japan'. © Japanmacroadvisors, September 2016; Ch5 data response adapted from article 'Disequilibrium in Pakistan's balance of trade' 13 January 2016 by Shahbaz Rana from Newspaper Express Tribune © Express Tribune; Figure 5.2 adapted from 'Pakistan Balance of Trade' source 'Pakistan Bureau of Statistics © Tradingeconomics.com; Figure 7.4 adapted from 'Market shares of selected companies in global banana exports by volume' © bananalink.org.uk; Figure 8.2 adapted from 'How to narrow the gap between rich and poor in Malaysia' Source: OECD, Household Income Survey 2014 (Malaysia), World Bank staff calculations © The World Bank Group; Figure 8.3 and Ch9 Data Response adapted from article 'Unclog Mumbai: You may like cars, but buses better' by Farhan Shaikh, Hindustan Times, 24 February 2016 © HT Media Limited; Figure 9.1 'India and China GDP Annual growth rate' © Trading Economics; Figure 9.2 'Pakistan and Indonesia Unemployment rates' © Trading Economics; Figure 10.2 'Chinese Real GDP Growth 1979–2013' © The International Monetary Fund (IMF)

Introduction

This workbook is designed to help you develop your knowledge of economics as you study your Cambridge International AS and A Level course. Working through it will help you feel more confident about what you need to know to be a successful economics student.

A unique feature of the workbook is that it includes a range of exercises in every chapter that will enable you to build up your skills and core knowledge of economics by seeing the ways in which these topics can subsequently be applied, analysed and evaluated. These core skills are also known as 'Assessment Objectives' and they are listed below for your reference:

- AO1 Knowledge and understanding **[K]**
- AO2 Application **[Ap]**
- AO3 Analysis **[A]**
- AO4 Evaluation **[E]**

The workbook is in two parts:

Part 1 covers the skills you need to develop when studying economics at AS and A Level.

Part 2 consists of ten chapters, five for AS Level and five for A Level, which directly draw upon the Cambridge syllabus. Each chapter contains exercises for you to work through and examples of typical exam-style questions: data response, essay and multiple choice questions. Many questions are new and up to date, having been specifically produced for this workbook. Some chapters also contain additional details about relevant economic issues and policies and how well-known economists have contributed to the subject.

This workbook is best used alongside the latest edition of the endorsed coursebook (Bamford, C.G. and Grant, S.J., *Cambridge International AS and A Level Economics*, 2015, ISBN 978-1-107-67951-1), and the revision guide (Grant, S.J., *Cambridge International AS and A Level Economics Revision Guide*, 2016, ISBN 978-1-316-63809-5).

Answers to the exam-style questions are provided online, as well as advice on how to tackle the various exercises.

How to use this book

This book is designed as a practical workbook to help you put into practice the knowledge and skills you have learnt as you progress through your Economics course.

Carefully aligned to the syllabus, the practice questions and exercises will help you to develop the key skills of an economist, so that you can become confident in applying these to reach reasoned conclusions about economic issues.

Learning outcomes – each chapter begins by outlining the key economic issues that you should have learnt for that topic on your course. The concepts listed here will inform the questions and exercises found in that chapter.

Learning outcomes

The exercises in this chapter will help you to practise what you have learnt about:

- the fundamental economic problem
- scarcity and the inevitability of choices that have to be made by individuals, firms and governments
- opportunity cost
- why the basic questions of what, how and for whom production takes place have to be addressed in all economies
- the meaning of the term 'ceteris paribus'
- what is meant by the margin and decision-making at the margin
- the importance of the time dimension in economics
- the difference between positive and normative statements
- what is meant by factors of production, namely land, labour, capital and enterprise and the role of enterprise in the modern economy
- what is meant by the division of labour
- how resources are allocated in market, planned and mixed economies
- issues of transition when central planning in an economy is reduced
- the characteristics of a production possibility curve and how opportunity cost can be applied
- the functions and characteristics of money and types of money
- how goods can be classified into free goods, private goods, public goods, merit goods and demerit goods
- the problems associated with information failure.

Key terms – a reminder of the key terms for each chapter topic as you work through the questions and exercises.

KEY TERMS

You should **know and understand** what is meant by the following key terms. These terms are defined in Chapter 1 of the course book.

Resources	Long run	Reallocation of resources	Non-rival
Wants	Very long run	Factor mobility	Quasi-public good
Scarcity	Positive statement	Economic growth	Free rider
Choice	Normative statement	Capital consumption	Merit good
Fundamental economic problem	Specialisation	Investment	Demerit good
Factors of production	Market	Developing economy	Information failure
Land	Division of labour	Money	Paternalism
Labour	Economic structure	Near money	Moral hazard
Capital	Economic system	Liquidity	Adverse selection
Enterprise/ Entrepreneur	Market economy	Liabilities	
Production	Command/planned economy	Private goods	
Consumption	Mixed economy	Excludability	
Opportunity cost	Market mechanism	Rivalry	
Short run	Production possibility curve	Public good	
		Non-excludable	

Tip – occasional tips are in place to help you approach trickier concepts and question types.

TIP
The stem of the question indicates absolute advantage in both products. Part (a) therefore requires an explanation of how comparative advantage applies.

Remember – the remember feature may offer additional context on a topic, refer you back to a relevant point within the coursebook, or help you to avoid common mistakes made.

REMEMBER
The content of this chapter is very important in the AS microeconomic syllabus; it also underpins much of the A Level syllabus.

Exercises – scaffolded exercises and activities at regular intervals throughout the workbook allow you to progress through the sections of your course and practice what you have learnt in a particular unit or chapter.

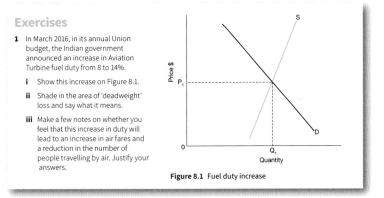

Exercises

1 In March 2016, in its annual Union budget, the Indian government announced an increase in Aviation Turbine fuel duty from 8 to 14%.

   i   Show this increase on Figure 8.1.

   ii Shade in the area of 'deadweight' loss and say what it means.

   iii Make a few notes on whether you feel that this increase in duty will lead to an increase in air fares and a reduction in the number of people travelling by air. Justify your answers.

Figure 8.1 Fuel duty increase

Exam-style questions – can be found at the end of each chapter in the workbook in the form of Multiple choice questions, Data response questions and Essay questions. These are designed so that you can check your understanding of particular questions as well as helping you to familiarise yourself with the style of questions you are likely to see in an exam.

Exam-style questions

Data response question

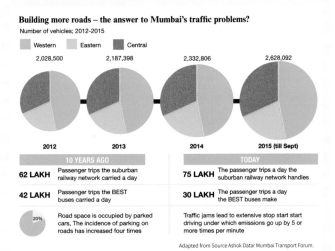

Building more roads – the answer to Mumbai's traffic problems?

Number of vehicles; 2012-2015

Figure 8.3 Number of vehicles used in Mumbai 2012–2015

Mumbai, India's largest city with around 13m people, has some of the most serious traffic congestion in the world. This is hardly surprising given that another 295,000 vehicles were added to Mumbai's streets in 2015. Chaos is inevitable as the city planners continue to give priority to private vehicles over public transport.

Most of those who use the roads for their daily commute either have their own cars and two-wheelers or use taxis and the iconic auto-rickshaws. These all fight for space along with trucks, especially in the evening peak period. The western suburbs, which have the most private vehicles, are worst affected.

Congestion resulting from increasing levels of car use tends to be a self-inflicted problem. Philipp Rode from the London School of Economics argues that the increase in vehicles in Mumbai is no different to that in most cities in developing economies – the problem is made worse by the compact nature of Mumbai and its high density of population, which make the city very vulnerable to the increasing flood of vehicles.

The city aims to improve its mobility by building even more new roads and flyovers which, according to local transport planner Priyanka Vasudevan, will only serve to induce more vehicle congestion. In his opinion, 'We need to rethink our approach to congestion and utilise the space that is available more effectively'.

Source: Hindustan Times, 24 February 2016 (adapted).

Multiple choice questions – at the end of each chapter you will find a series of multiple choice questions which relate to the topic you have just covered in the chapter. Practicing these will help you to check your understanding at regular intervals through the book.

Multiple choice questions

1 As an economics student, you decide to revise for your examination rather than play with your friends in a cricket team. What is the opportunity cost of your decision?

   A You might get a higher mark in the examination.

   B Your cricket team lose the match.

   C The enjoyment you would get if you had played in the match.

   D The money you have saved by staying at home.

Think like an economist – this feature is designed to contextualise the topics you have learnt in each chapter within real-world economic scenarios. Each of these deals with a key economic issue complete with a related economic myth, a lead economist in the field and a key economic policy to consider.

Think like an economist

Key economic myth

Governments should know what policies to use in pursuit of their macroeconomic aims and what the outcomes of such policies should be.

You might think that with an army of economists and a mass of data, governments should know how to meet their macroeconomic objectives. Nothing could be further from the truth. The reality is that macroeconomic problems are not discrete. Conflicts arise in meeting aims and in deciding what policies are going to be most effective. There is the additional problem of unforeseen exogenous shocks to the economy, such as the financial collapse in 2008 that fuelled a global recession.

Key economist

J.K. Galbraith, the Canadian-born economist, was arguably the most well-known American economist of the 20th century. He was controversial through his support of post-Keynesian economics at a time when monetarism and supply-side policies were largely the order of the day. He was also controversial in the way that he made economics relevant to the many political crises that faced the US economy.

Improve your answer – based on advice and strategies provided, this feature provides you with an opportunity to reflect on a given answer and think about how it could be made better. This process can then be applied to your own work as you progress through your course and the resource.

Improve your answer

Read the question and answer below and see how you can improve it using the suggestions that follow.

Question

a *Explain the impact on the market of a subsidy paid to wheat producers.* **[8]**

b *Comment on the view of the Asian Development Bank that 'Targeted food subsidies would help South Asia cope with future food price spikes'.* **[12]**

a A subsidy is a payment made directly to a producer, in this case, the wheat farmer. The payments come direct from the government or in the case of Europe, the European Commission through its controversial Common Agricultural Policy. Subsidies are paid to agricultural producers in developed as well as in emerging and developing economies. Their impact on the market is shown on the diagram below.

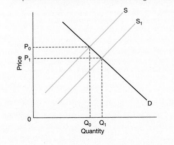

Figure 3.5 The impact of a subsidy on the market

Part 1

1.1 Developing skills

This part covers the range of skills that underpin the Cambridge International AS and A Level Economics syllabus. The aim is to progressively get you to think like an economist through being able to use what is often referred to as 'the economist's tool kit'.

The following sections are covered:

- Core skills for an economist: knowledge and understanding; application; analysis and evaluation.
- How to tackle the various types of question and apply the appropriate skills.
- Numerical data – an overview of the skills that you need.
- Diagrams – how these are used in economics as a means of explaining economic concepts.
- How to write clear convincing economic arguments.

Each section contains advice that is appropriate for AS and A Level students.

Acquiring knowledge and developing understanding skills

Why knowledge and understanding are important in economics

Like any academic subject, the starting point when studying economics is to acquire essential knowledge. This knowledge is the core of the subject and is progressively acquired as you work through the five sections of the AS and A Level syllabus.

Much of the knowledge can be obtained from the many 'key terms' set out in the various chapters of the course book. You should be able to define these key terms in an exact way.

Understanding is something that you can develop from this knowledge.

How to recognise when knowledge and understanding is required

The directive or command word of a question should make this clear.

You will always find it useful to define any key terms at the start of an answer. But be careful to make sure you can do this correctly.

A few examples of directive or command words requiring knowledge and understanding are:

Define	:	Give the (exact) meaning of …
Describe	:	Give the main features of …
Outline	:	Describe the key points without going into detail.
State	:	Give a clear, brief answer with no need to provide anything else.
Illustrate	:	Use examples; use a diagram.

How to show that you have a knowledge and understanding of economics

This is the first stage in developing the skills that will help you to think like an economist.

A few positive steps you can take are:

- be clear and precise when defining key terms
- avoid long drawn out definitions and vague descriptions
- try to show that you really understand what you are writing about and why it is important.

Some questions, especially in data response questions, may simply ask for a definition. Essay questions may use key terms, in which case, is often useful to define these before attempting more detailed application and analysis.

The table below gives some examples where students sometimes get confused over the meaning of key terms. You will find it useful to keep referring back to it. The terms are broadly set out in the order in which they appear in the syllabus.

Key term	Often confused with
wants	needs
public goods	merit goods
elastic	inelastic
price	cost
movement along demand/supply curves	shifts of demand/supply curves
maximum prices	minimum prices
direct taxes	indirect taxes
inflation	deflation
balance of trade	balance of payments
exchange rate	interest rate
terms of trade	balance of trade
trade creation	trade diversion
fiscal policies	monetary policies
expenditure switching policies	expenditure dampening policies
external costs/benefits	social costs/benefits
substitution effect	income effect
monopolistic competition	monopoly
horizontal integration	vertical integration
equity	equality
income	wealth
economic growth	economic development
autonomous investment	induced investment
multiplier	accelerator

Table 0.1 Key terms

Applying knowledge and understanding

Why application is important in economics

Economics was once described as the 'dismal science', most likely because it was often difficult to see how the economist's language of terms, concepts and theories had any real-world relevance. This criticism is not one that can be made of the subject in the 21st century.

The main reason for this modern view is that economics has substantial relevance in the complex, uncertain, global economy. The concepts and simple models that make up the subject form the way in which economists view the world around us. Economists try to simplify and make sense of what they see in terms of these tools. In short, the particular value of economics is through its application in making sense of an ever-wider range of micro- and macroeconomic problems and issues.

How to recognise when application is required

Unlike other skills, there are only a few specific command or directive words, other than 'apply' and 'explain', that indicate that some application is required. These words are widely used.

The wording of the question should help you recognise when application is required.

For example:

> **'Use the information** in table 1 to explain …'
> **'What evidence** is there to indicate that …'
> **'With the aid of a diagram**, apply …'
> **'How can** (concept *x*) be used to explain …'
> **'Distinguish** between … and …'
> **'Calculate** …'

How to show that you can apply a knowledge and understanding of economics

There are various ways in which you can do this.

In data response questions, an obvious way is to explicitly use the text or data provided in your answer whilst making reference to the concept or issue involved.

In essay questions, there is wider scope including:

- making a brief summary of a concept or key term and then specifically applying it to the topic of the question
- for more open-ended questions, drawing upon what you might have read either in a textbook or newspaper or some digital resource and applying this original knowledge to the question.

Developing analysis skills

Why analysis is important in economics?

The analysis of economic problems and issues is central to what economics is all about. Professional economists such as those working for banks, international organisations and especially the media, set about analysing a wide range of micro- and macroeconomic situations. Developing this skill is one that will help enhance your more detached understanding of economics and increase your confidence when preparing for examinations.

'Analysis' is concerned with the ability to dissect or separate an issue or problem into its basic elements or components. This enables you to show the essence of what it consists of, whilst avoiding unnecessary detail. This last point is very important otherwise you will struggle to give relevant answers.

In analysing a particular issue, the subject matter of economics provides you with a range of tools.

These are:

- a range of micro- and macroeconomic concepts

- corresponding theories that can be applied to compare theory and practice

- data that can be used to investigate a particular issue.

Making the transition from understanding and describing an economic issue is not easy, nor is getting to grips with writing in an analytical way. Both can be achieved as you develop your knowledge of economics and become more confident in understanding what is involved.

How to recognise when analysis is required

Many economics questions require analysis. The directive or command word of the question can be a clue as to when analysis is required.

An obvious way of recognising when analysis is required is where the question says 'analyse'. So:

Analyse   :   Set out the main points and show how they link and connect.

Other command words involving the same skill are:

Explain   :   Give clear reasons or make clear the meaning, using examples and theory where appropriate remember that this is also a directive word for application skills.

Compare   :   Explain similarities as well as differences (between two concepts).

How to show that you can analyse economic issues, policies and arguments

This skill requires practice, whether through homework tasks, the exercises and questions in this workbook or drafting answers to examination questions. It is not something that you can develop overnight. So, practice is the key.

The most important advice is to always have the following in mind:

- **Why?**

- **How?**

- **Therefore...**

Think about these questions all of the time you are writing. This will enable you to 'link' individual sentences together – this is how to write in a critical, analytical way. The diagram below will help you understand this point.

Figure 0.1 Linking individual sentences in a critical analytical way

Here is an example of what this means:

Question: **Analyse** *how fiscal policy can be used to increase the level of activity in an economy.*

Below is an example of an analytical response:

Fiscal policy is widely used by governments when seeking to reflate the economy and reduce the problem of rising unemployment.

(How?)

It is a policy that involves changes to taxation or government spending or to both.

(Why?)

An expansionary fiscal policy can increase the level of aggregate demand through a reduction in taxation or an increase in government spending.

(Why?)

Such measures increase consumption, one of the components of aggregate demand, by individuals and businesses.

(Why?)

A reduction in, for example, a general sales tax, increases disposable income; an increase in government spending on roads or constructing new state schools for example, provides a boost to firms involved in such work.

(Therefore)

Outcome

This should increase aggregate demand and the level of activity in the economy since firms will buy more supplies and take on more workers to meet the increased demand.

Developing evaluation skills

Why evaluation is important in economics

Have you noticed how economists often disagree? This is because, unlike maths for example, economics is not an exact science – there can be different interpretations of a particular economic issue or alternative policies being put forward to deal with it. This is why, at AS/A Level, developing the skills necessary to be able to evaluate or make a judgement is important.

Let us consider two issues you may have studied. These are tariffs (AS) and market failure as a consequence of traffic congestion (A Level).

Tariffs are imposed, rightly or wrongly, to protect an economy from what might be seen to be unfair competition in international trade. Some economists argue that tariffs are necessary to protect sunrise and sunset industries and to reduce pressures on the balance of trade in goods. Others argue that tariffs are counter to the principle of comparative advantage and the resulting benefits that can be gained through specialisation in the global economy.

Traffic congestion is a classic example of market failure. All economists would agree on this point. Where they disagree is what to do about it. Some economists urge intervention through policies such as increased restrictions on vehicle use or greater public transport (mass transit) subsidies. Other economists promote a market solution through a policy of road pricing.

In both examples, therefore, there are alternative viewpoints. Their evaluation involves studying the evidence available and putting forward what is seen as the 'best' policy outcome.

Here are a few useful tips:

- It is important that any evaluation of a problem or issue is based on good quality information. This is sometimes difficult as there may be no precedent or no empirical (real-world) evidence to support a particular policy approach.

- Evaluation can also be derived from recognised economic principles or concepts, such as those you study at AS/A Level. Economic theories have often stood the test of time and can be used to 'benchmark' real situations.

- Avoid making rash judgements that are not based on quality information or economic principles. At least 99% of the time, these will be meaningless, purely a matter of biased personal opinion.

How to recognise where evaluation is required

This is relatively straightforward since evaluation is clearly flagged up by the command or directive word in a question.

The most common such word is '**discuss**'. This invites you to look at both sides of an economic issue, policy or argument.

A good way of knowing how to discuss an economic issue is to think about the 'two-handed economist'. Typically, economists often argue 'on the one hand' but 'on the other hand' when considering something. The aim is to give a balanced answer. A very good answer, if valid, would go that bit further and conclude by making clear which side (or hand) has most credibility **based on the evidence in your answer**. This is particularly valuable at A Level since your knowledge and understanding of economics will be that bit greater.

Other command words, mainly in A Level questions, requiring an evaluation in an answer include:

Assess	:	Look at the respective arguments and make a judgement (based on what you have written) of how important something is.
To what extent	:	Look at reasons for and against and come to a conclusion based on what you believe to be the strongest side of the argument.
Evaluate	:	Again, consider the respective arguments but make some deliberate attempt to weight them in terms of their importance.
Comment	:	This may sometimes require you to only make an evaluation of one rather than both sides of an economic argument. If so, you need to be clear why you have rejected other arguments whilst giving a reasoned opinion
Consider	:	Give your thoughts about the statement with some justification.

7

How to show that you can evaluate economic issues, policies and arguments

Making an evaluation in an answer is the final challenge. In general, there are two main ways you can do this. These are:

i To round off your answer with a concluding paragraph or two. You can do this by summing up what you have found, for and against, and then make a final statement such as:

'From the evidence, it is clear that … is a better policy than …'

'There is no particular evidence for one policy over another. The best approach is that of using a mixture of policies.'

'In the short term, a policy of … is most likely to succeed but in the long term …'

What you have said earlier really does have to consider the two respective sides of the issue, policies or argument.

ii Evaluation can also be incorporated at various points in the full answer to a question. This is more of a challenge but is evidenced in the way in which you write or structure an answer to a question.

To be effective, such an answer needs to have a clear linkage between the points made, as distinct from a set of discrete points. It should also periodically include an evaluative sentence once linked points have been set out. For example:

'These policies are clearly relevant since they are widely used.'

'It is therefore debatable whether there really is any one solution to this problem.'

'Other approaches need to be considered because of the problems that have so far been identified.'

Either way of incorporating evaluation is acceptable. As previously mentioned, the key thing is to have included appropriate underpinning content in your answer.

1.2 How to approach different types of questions in Economics

This section provides advice on how to approach three different types of question in Economics. These are:

- Multiple choice
- Data response
- Essay

How to approach multiple choice questions

Some students mistakenly believe that multiple choice questions are easier than data response or essay questions. Do not make this mistake. Multiple choice questions often require you to be familiar with the full range of subject content and the skills that go with it. The best advice is to familiarise yourself with multiple choice questions by incorporating them into your regular study of the various topics in the syllabus.

Multiple choice questions are likely to consist of:

- a stem that states what is required

- four possible choices or responses: A, B, C, D.

A simple strategy to help you pick the correct answer is:

1 Carefully read the question and each of the four possible answers.

2 Cross out any choices that seem incorrect.

3 Go back to the question and look for any 'key terms'; make sure you understand what they mean.

4 Choose the answer that makes most sense.

5 Make a guess if you are still unsure.

An alternative approach is to treat each choice as being 'true' or 'false'. The correct answer is the one that is deemed to be 'most true'. Those that are eliminated are therefore 'false' or 'not as true' as the one you have selected. An example of this type of question is below.

Question: An economy is seeking to increase its aggregate supply. Which of these measures is most likely to produce short-term growth?

   A   increased expenditure on secondary education

   B   easing controls on migrant workers

   C   privatisation of water supply

   D   new skills training for redundant mineworkers

Comment: All choices are true and will increase aggregate supply over time. The one which will be most likely to happen quickly is B; the other three choices are likely to take longer to increase aggregate supply. The reference to 'short-term' in the stem is the prompt for the best answer.

Question: Market research by a food manufacturer showed that its product *x* was an inferior good and that it was a close substitute to a competitor's product, good *y*.

Given this information, which of the estimates below would support the market research?

	Income elasticity of demand for good X	Cross elasticity of demand for good *x* with respect to the price of good *y*
A	−1.5	−0.8
B	−1.5	+0.8
C	+1.5	−0.8
D	+1.5	+0.8

Comment: An inferior good has a negative income elasticity of demand. So, options C and D can be discounted. A substitute good has a positive cross elasticity of demand with respect to a change in the price of another good. Therefore, option A can now be discounted. The answer is B.

Question: Assume an open economy. An increase in government spending has resulted in an increase in national income of $1000 million. Of this, consumers save $50 million, $150 million m is paid to the government in taxes and $50 million is spent on imports. Calculate the value of the multiplier.

A 0.4   **B** 0.25   **C** 2.5   **D** 4

Comment: From the data, it is necessary to calculate each of the mps, mrt and mpm. The multiplier is then calculated as $\frac{1}{\text{mps} + \text{mrt} + \text{mpm}}$. This gives $\frac{1}{0.05 + 0.15 + 0.05}$, namely $\frac{1}{0.25}$. This gives a multiplier of 4. So D is the correct answer.

Question: The data below relates to the Human Development Index (HDI) for a developing economy over a five-year period. What can you conclude from the data?

Year	1	2	3	4	5
GNI per head Year 1 = 100	100	110	120	118	118
Life expectancy in years	68	68	69	69	68
Educational dimension	12	11.5	12.5	13	13

Table 0.2 Human Development Index (HDI) for a developing economy over a five-year period

A The level of development in year 4 was below that in year 3.

B Economic growth was 10% between years 2 and 3 with no growth between years 4 and 5.

C The level of development improved from year 2 to year 3.

D No conclusions can be made on the change in the level of development.

Comment: The three variables shown in the table are used to estimate the HDI for an economy. D can therefore be discounted. The calculation in option B should be made next. Economic growth as measured by the change in GNI per head was just over 9% and not 10% although there was no growth between years 4 and 5.

This can now be discounted. Looking at year 4, one variable increased, one fell and one remained the same. So, in these terms, option A is not correct as the % in secondary education increased. This leaves option C. Between years 2 and 3, the values of each three variables increased so this is the correct response.

How to approach data response questions

In data response questions, the term 'data' is applied in a broad sense and can take various forms including:

- text that includes a table of numerical data or a diagram containing numerical data
- text with some data incorporated
- text only.

The principle behind such questions is that they are designed to test your ability to recognise and understand how economic concepts apply in real-world situations. You may also be required to use basic data handling skills in order to answer some of the questions.

Questions may be derived from up-to-date articles in the media, including newspapers, government reports and internet sources. The scope is global, although no other specific knowledge of the context is required.

Some data response questions may have many parts; whereas others only have a few. For questions with fewer parts remember that your answer is likely to need a bit more depth, but be careful not to write more than is needed for each answer.

It might sound obvious, but allow some time to read and digest the data and all parts of the question so that you have a better understanding of what is required in each answer before you start writing.

A recommended strategy that you can adopt is:

i   Scan the text and any numerical information in order to get a feel for the topic; look at the title and where the material has come from.

ii   Underline any key terms and key issues in the text.

iii Look at any numerical data and make sure that you know what it means.

iv   Read the questions, noting the command words and marks that are allocated as these will give you a strong indication as to how much you should write.

Two examples of data response questions are shown below. Using the guidance provided, why not see if you can write a good answer?

Question

Turkey's economic policies

Key issue of structural reforms to increase growth.

KEY TERMS

inflation

current account deficit

fiscal policy

potential growth

interest rate

saving

Changes in consumer prices in 2014 are higher than in 2013.

Extract 1: Turkey's medium-term programme

In a press statement in 2014, Turkey's minister in charge of the economy, Ali Babacan, introduced Turkey's medium-term programme (MTP) for the period 2015–2017. He stated that the first priority of the MTP is solving the problem of inflation, second is the current account deficit and third is structural reforms.

Tight fiscal policy will be pursued in order to reach Turkey's goals of lower inflation and a reduced current account deficit. Structural reforms are important to increase Turkey's potential growth, the minister said.

He announced that the inflation rate is expected to fall from 9.4% in 2014 to 6.3% in 2015 and 5.0% by 2017. The minister also stated that the unemployment rate is expected to drop from 9.6% in 2014 to 9.1% by 2017.

As the United States (US) economy recovers, the US central bank is expected to increase interest rates, causing the US dollar to continue to rise. The outcome of these policies might be harmful for Turkey's economy.

The minister claimed that Turkey's macroeconomic policies were already increasing saving in the economy and reducing consumer credit. By 2017, domestic savings are expected to rise to 15% of national income.

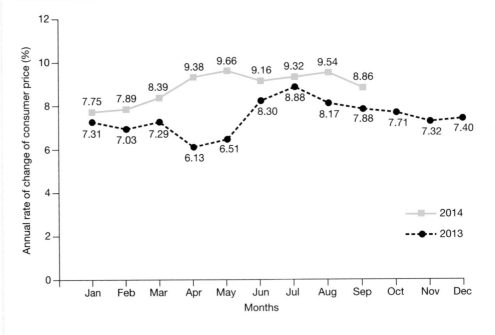

Figure 0.2 Turkey's consumer price inflation rate, January 2013–September 2014

12

	2012	2013
Exports of goods	163,221	163,371
Imports of goods	−228,552	−243,394
Services	22,562	23,131
Income	−7,161	−9,355
Current transfers	1,433	1,181

Balance on current account is in deficit (i.e. negative) in 2012 and 2013.

Deficit increases in 2013.

Table 0.3 Turkey's balance of payments current account, 2012–2013 (US$ million)

a   What happened to the balance on Turkey's current account between 2012 and 2013? **[2]**

b   Use a production possibility curve diagram to show the intended outcome of the structural reforms in Turkey. **[2]**

c   With the help of a demand and supply diagram, show how the expected change in US interest rates was likely to cause the US dollar 'to continue to rise'. **[2]**

d   Consider whether the outcome of the interest rate changes in the US was likely to be 'harmful for Turkey's economy'. **[4]**

e   Explain **two** factors that determine how the increase in consumer prices between 2013 and 2014 shown in Figure. 0.3 might affect the total value of Turkey's exports. **[4]**

f   Discuss how 'tight fiscal policy' could be expected to help Turkey achieve the first priority of the MTP, and consider how effective this is likely to be. **[6]**

Cambridge International AS and A Level Economics 9708 Paper 22 Q1 May/June 2016.

With respect to the questions:

a   The answer is deduced from your scan of the data in Table 0.3.

b   On a PPC diagram, show how it changes through the outcome of structural reforms (potential growth). Remember to label the axes correctly.

c   The fourth paragraph says 'the US central bank is expected to increase interest rates' and 'the US dollar to continue to rise'. In other words, the US dollar is expected to appreciate against other currencies, including Turkey's. How does this affect the demand for the US dollar? Show this on a diagram and give a brief explanation. Remember to label the axes correctly.

d   How will the appreciation of the US dollar affect Turkey's economy? What about the likely effect on Turkey's export prices and the price of imports from the US? Conclude by saying whether these effects will be 'harmful' for Turkey's economy.

e   Figure 0.3 shows an annual increase of around 7–10% in consumer prices in Turkey. How might this increase affect prices and hence the value of Turkey's exports? Or will it?

f   Make sure you are clear on what is meant by 'tight fiscal policy'. Define it and then, as stated in the first paragraph, explain and then discuss whether such a policy is likely to be effective in 'solving the problem of inflation'. An AD/AS diagram will enhance your answer.

Are increasing prices due to increasing demand or to a lack of supply? Link between housing and growth.

KEY TERMS

interest rates

investment

employment

demand

supply

consumer spending

export-led growth

Question

Housing and Economic Growth in the UK

In 2013 a press article reported that 'there has been a marked improvement in the housing market'. Potential buyers of housing had been encouraged because the central bank had fixed interest rates at an all-time low and there was also a government scheme designed to give help to people wishing to buy property. The scheme meant that buyers did not have to find such a large deposit.

This caused a positive outcome for the construction industry, with investment and employment rising. However, it pushed up property prices.

In 2013 the average price of a house was seven times the average wage. A study recommended that the central bank should take steps to prevent house prices rising by more than 5% a year and should limit the amount people could borrow, relative to their incomes. There should be regional variations to this limit, as property prices do not increase at the same rate in every region.

However, a deputy governor of the central bank said that limiting price rises would not solve the cause of the problem, which was the lack of new property development. He found it surprising that the study chose to focus exclusively on the demand side when the underlying problem was one of supply.

An economist said that the most effective intervention a government can make in the housing market is to relax the planning system and make it easier and cheaper to build more homes. Increased supply, leading to lower prices, would encourage demand. Others said that 'although there is talk of a large rise in the price of houses, it is not uniform throughout the country and trying to influence the basic laws of supply and demand is not the right way of tackling the problem'.

The buying of housing gives rise to increased consumer spending and some argue that this helps the economy. Although policies by the government and the central bank had increased consumer demand and spending, such expenditure is quite different from the export-led growth model preferred by the government. Analysts suggested that the demand and supply conditions causing the current situation cannot last forever. When they end, the effect on the housing market (which by then will have many people with very high debts) will be very bad for the economy. This can be seen in countries such as Spain and the Netherlands, where property values are in decline.

Source: The Times, 14 September 2013.

a Identify two government policies in the article that could encourage an increase in aggregate demand. **[2]**

b The article states that there has been a 'marked improvement in the housing market'.

Using the article and your own knowledge, explain how an economy might benefit from an 'improvement in the housing market'. **[5]**

c Using the evidence in the article, assess whether it contradicts the view that an increase in house prices is an improvement for an economy. **[6]**

d The article contrasts a model of an increase in growth through consumer spending with a model of an increase in growth through exports.

Choose two macroeconomic aims of a government and discuss how the two growth models might have different effects on those aims. **[7]**

Cambridge International AS and A Level Economics 9708 Paper 42 Q1 May/June 2016.

This question contains micro and macroeconomic issues.

With respect to the questions:

a The most obvious answers are contained in the first paragraph, although there are others later in the text. For each policy, say what it is and how it can lead to an increase in aggregate demand.

b The term 'marked improvement in the housing market' is in the first sentence. (This means there is a positive situation in this market.) You therefore need to explain how this can impact upon the economy as a whole, particularly in terms of increasing economic growth (see title and key issues box).

c This question requires you to look at evidence, in the last two paragraphs especially, as to why the increase in house prices is not necessarily a good thing for the economy and UK residents. A solid conclusion should be made from your evidence.

d The first thing to do is to choose two macroeconomic aims (reducing unemployment and improving the current account balance for example). Then consider increased consumer spending and export-led growth and explain how they are likely to affect your chosen macroeconomic aims. Make clear any different effects on these aims, with a clear final evaluation.

How to approach essay questions

Essay questions can take various forms and may consist of two-parts or have more than one requirement.

When deciding which question or questions to answer, it is important that you feel confident in being able to answer both parts effectively and not just the most straightforward part.

How to dissect an essay question

All essay questions, whether structured or unstructured, can be broken down into two components. These are:

i Command or directive words. These relate to the assessment objectives and provide a clear indication of the style of answer that is required.

ii Content words and phrases. These draw upon the subject topics of the syllabus and may also provide an applied context for the questions.

The three examples below give you a simple way of how to approach this type of question; there is one AS Level question and two A Level questions.

Using the guidance provided why not see if you can write a good answer?

Question: Use examples to illustrate the difference between private goods and public goods and explain why only private goods will be supplied in a free market economy. **[8]**

Cambridge International AS and A Level Economics 9708 Paper 22 Q2a June 2016.

The question has two command words. These are:

illustrate	explain

This indicates that you need to use examples to show the difference. **[knowledge and understanding]**

Say why. **[application]**

There are two content requirements. These are:

| Public goods | Only private goods will be |
| Private goods | supplied in a free market economy |

Give the characteristics of private goods and public goods, with appropriate examples.

Say why private goods will be provided and public goods will not be provided in a free market economy.

Other points to note:

- The question initially requires 'differences' to be understood; contrasts can be made by giving the characteristics of each in turn.
- Make sure your answer has examples of both private goods and public goods.
- There is no need to write a lot about a free market economy – a simple statement will suffice.
- Make clear why only private goods will be provided in a free market economy, whilst saying why public goods will not be provided (the 'free rider' issue is important).
- Provide a balanced answer to both parts of the question.

Question: *Governments want to increase the standard of living in their country.*

Discuss whether the indicators used to measure the standard of living are reliable and consider what policies a government might use to increase the standard of living in its country. **[25]**

Cambridge International AS and A Level Economics 9708 Paper 42 Q7 February/March 2016.

The question has two separate requirements with the following command words. These are:

| Discuss | Consider |

Make some judgement.

Say which policies are likely to be best

There are two content requirements. These are:

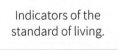

| Indicators of the | Policies to increase the |
| standard of living. | standard of living. |

Monetary, e.g. GDP per head and non-monetary indicators such as HDI, HPI and MEW – concentrate on the reliability of each indicator.

Trade policy, policies designed to increase investment and FDI and debt reduction. How such policies can increase standard of living.

Other points to note:

- Don't lose sight of the question. There is a lot of content in this essay so avoid too much detail.
- For each indicator mentioned, make sure you make a judgement on its likely statistical reliability; try to say which one you believe to be most reliable.
- Use economic analysis to explain how each of the policies might increase the standard of living; try to say which might be best.
- Use examples from your own country or one that is known to you.

Question: *The traditional theory of the firm assumes a single objective for the firm, namely the maximisation of profit.*

Discuss how the objective in the traditional theory may be varied in different market structures. **[13]**

Cambridge International AS and A Level Economics 9708 Paper 42 Q5b May/June 2016.

This question has just one command word:

Discuss

Look at the case for and against
and make a final judgement.

The content requirement links two parts of the syllabus,

Profit maximisation
objective and other
objectives of firms

and

Different market structures

Brief analysis of profit maximisation objective and its place in the theory of the firm; other objectives including behavioural approaches.

Look at main market structures (perfect competition, monopolistic competition, oligopoly and monopoly) and say which of the objectives are most likely.

Other points to note:

- There is no need to explain the respective market structures; the point of the question is about how the various objectives of firms might apply in different market structures.

- Your final paragraph should make clear whether there is a link and if so, which objectives are likely to be most prevalent in which market structure.

- The cases of perfect competition and monopoly are the easiest to consider; monopolistic competition and oligopoly are more problematic.

Being confident when using numerical economic data is an important skill in economics. It will help you when answering data response questions; it is also very helpful when you are studying certain economic concepts, particularly in macroeconomics, since many of these concepts have been developed empirically through the use of economic data.

Some of the skills you need to have are:

- to be able to scan a table of data or a diagram in order to pick out the main features

- to know how averages are calculated and what they mean

- to be able to pick out the main trend or trends in time-series data and know what is the rate of change

- to understand how index numbers are calculated and how they can be used to identify a trend or rate of change in data.

As well as these skills, there are times when you need to stand back from the data and ask yourself 'How accurate or how reliable are these data?' Particularly when looking at data from developing economies, this is a key issue; data collection methods are likely to be less robust than in developed economies.

The key message is 'be positive'. Do not be afraid of numerical data. The examples that follow will give you an indication of the sort of tasks you are likely to come across in your course. Look at each and see if you can complete the data handling tasks.

Example 1:

Brazil	6.5
Russia	5.2
India[1]	3.4
China[2]	4.1
South Africa	25.1

Notes: [1]subsidiary activity included
         [2]urban areas only.

Source: BRICS Joint Statistical Publication, 2015.

Table 0.4 Unemployment rate (%) for the BRICS countries (Brazil, Russia, India and China), 2013–2014

A simple average for the five countries is calculated by adding up the five unemployment rates and dividing by 5. This gives an average of 8.9%.

But if you look at this average and then compare it with the actual data, it does not seem at all representative.

So ask yourself:

i   Why is this?

ii How might a better measure of average be calculated?

iii Are the data really comparable?

Example 2: *Gross Domestic Product (GDP) of the BRIC countries 2010–2016, US$ billion*

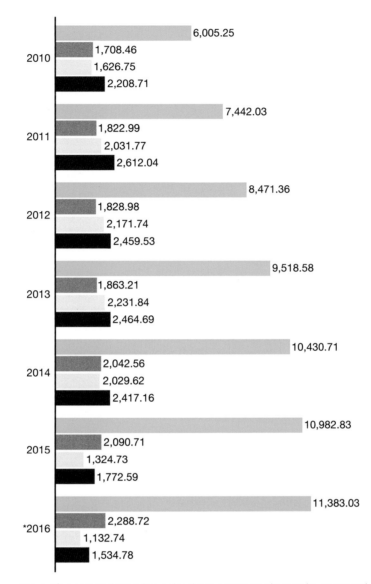

Notes: * forecast. In descending order, the countries are China, India, Russia and Brazil.

Source: Statistica.com, 2016.

Figure 0.3 Gross Domestic Product (GDP) of the BRIC countries 2010–2016, US$ billion

To scan this data, take each country in turn and make a note of how their GDP has changed over the seven-year period.

You should then be able to:

i Say which countries have experienced an annual increase in GDP.

ii Describe the change in India's GDP.

iii Say which country has experienced the greatest change in its GDP.

iv Note why the data for 2015 and 2016 is a forecast or estimate.

v Consider the accuracy of the data.

Example 3: *Distribution of employed persons by major industries in Pakistan in 2013–2014*

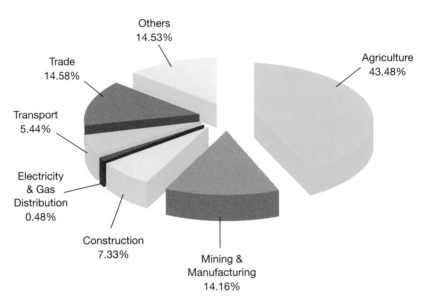

Source: Population, Labour Force and Employment, Ministry of Labour, 2015.

Figure 0.4 Pie chart showing distribution of employed persons by major industries in Pakistan in 2013–2014

Pie charts are a useful way of visually showing the relative importance of each category within a set of data. Each 'slice' shows this and its size is determined in relation to the total of 360°. The respective percentages are usually shown.

It should be very clear as to:

i which industry is the main employer

ii how to calculate the relative size of the service sector.

Example 4: *Annual change in consumer Price Index (CPI) from previous year for BRICS countries*

	2009	2010	2011	2012	2013	2014
Brazil	4.3	5.9	6.5	5.8	5.9	6.4
Russia	11.7	6.9	8.4	5.1	6.8	7.8
India[1]	10.8	12.0	8.9	9.3	10.9	6.3
China	−0.7	3.3	5.4	2.6	2.6	2.0
South Africa	7.1	4.3	5.0	5.6	5.7	6.1

Note: [1]for industrial workers only.

Source: BRICS Joint Statistical Publication, 2015.

Table 0.5

The data refer to the percentage change in the Consumer Price Index (CPI) of each country 'from the previous year'. This could be confusing as, with the exception of China in 2009, the CPI has increased annually in each of the five countries. Overall, therefore, consumer prices have increased year on year, although the rate of change may have varied.

It is useful to look at the overall trend by showing the data in the form of an index. By taking 2008 as a base year, this is given an index of 100. For Brazil, 2009 becomes an index of 104.3; 2010 becomes 104.3 × 1.059 = 110.5 and so on. **This conversion makes it much easier to see how the level of the CPI has changed over the period.**

You should now be able to say:

i   which country had the largest increase in its CPI

ii which country had the smallest increase in its CPI

iii which country had the most volatile changes in its CPI

iv what happened to the CPI in Brazil (say) between 2010 and 2011 and between 2011 and 2012.

1.4 Using diagrams effectively

Diagrams are widely used in economics to aid the explanation of a particular concept or issue.

The general advice is:

- Use a diagram where it will improve the quality of your answer, work or homework.
- If adding an explanation, try to use any terms that you have included on your diagram.
- It is useful to label diagrams as 'Figure 1', etc. with a title and refer to them in this way.
- Makes sure you label the axes correctly.
- It is sound practice to label the origin '0'.
- Take care to draw the diagram as accurately as you can.

Interpreting diagrams

The skill when interpreting diagrams is to do this in a systematic way. This will enable you to maximise the explanation that a diagram can provide within the body of your work. However, do bear in mind the earlier advice.

Below are two examples of questions where there is an opportunity for a diagram or diagrams to improve your answer. See if you can write out the suggested interpretation.

Example 1: *The government has embarked on an economic policy that is designed to provide a fiscal boost to reduce unemployment. Comment on whether this is likely to be successful.* **[12]**

The diagram below can be incorporated into an answer to this question:

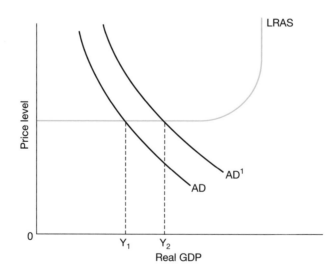

Figure 0.5 An increase in aggregate demand

The following stages can be followed to give an interpretation:

i   Briefly explain the nature and shape of the AD and LRAS curves.

ii Identify the initial equilibrium position.

iii Explain the effect of the increase in government funding on AD and how this is shown on the diagram.

iv Identify the new equilibrium position.

v Compare this with the original equilibrium.

vi Explain the wider macroeconomic implications of the changes.

Example 2: *Explain why in monopolistic competition, there is an inefficient allocation of resources.* **[12]**

The two diagrams below can be incorporated into an answer to this question.

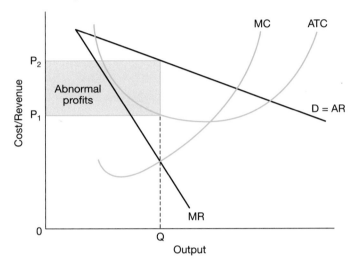

Figure 0.6 Monopolistic competition – short-run equilibrium

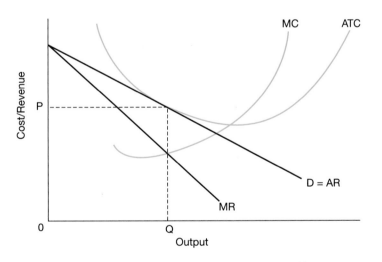

Figure 0.7 Monopolistic competition – long-run equilibrium

The following stages can be followed to give an interpretation:

i Refer to Figure 0.6 as the short-run equilibrium position.

ii Explain this and say how the firm is making abnormal profits.

iii Continue by saying why the equilibrium position is inefficient.

iv Move on to Figure 0.7; explain why there are no longer abnormal profits in the long run.

v Say why the long-run equilibrium position is also inefficient and what this means.

Useful diagrams

The following is a list of diagrams that are useful for describing or explaining concepts, although this list is by no means exhaustive. Alongside are references as to where they occur in the third edition of the course book.

Make sure you are familiar with each, and importantly, how they can be explained in words.

AS Level

Production possibility curves – how to show a movement within, along and a shift in the PPC (pages 27–31).

Demand and supply curves – a movement along each (pages 40–43).

Price inelastic and price elastic demand curves (pages 45–46).

Price inelastic and price elastic supply curves (pages 53–54).

Market equilibrium (pages 55–56).

Shifts in market demand and supply curves (pages 57–62).

Consumer and producer surplus (pages 63–64).

Effects of maximum and minimum price control (page 69).

Effects of introducing an indirect tax and subsidy (pages 71–73).

Aggregate demand and aggregate supply curves (pages 81–84).

Shifts in aggregate demand and aggregate supply curves (pages 87–90).

Exchange rate determination (pages 95–100).

Absolute and comparative advantage (pages 102–103).

Effect of imposing a tariff (page 108).

A Level

Productive efficiency (page 131).

Negative and positive externality (page 137).

Indifference curves and the effects of price and income changes (pages 148–149).

Firm costs of production (pages 152 and 155).

Perfect competition (page 164).

Monopolistic competition (page 166).

Monopoly and natural monopoly (page 170–171).

Kinked demand curve (page 183).

Deadweight loss (page 191).

Use of indirect taxation to combat negative externalities (page 192).

Use of a subsidy to increase external benefits (page 196).

Individual's labour supply curve (page 205).

Transfer earnings and economic rent (page 210).

Economic growth in terms of PPC and AD/AS (pages 219–220).

Changes in AD and effect on output (pages 244 and 249–252).

Money supply and the rate of interest (pages 257–258).

economic arguments

First, make sure you understand the 'How to show …', sub-sections in the section on 'acquiring knowledge and developing understanding skills' as well as the section on 'how to approach essay questions'.

In particular, the command word or words in a question will give you a clue as to what type of written answer is required. For example, is the answer to be written as an explanation (application) or an evaluation? It is very important before you start writing that you know what style of answer is required.

Here are a few useful tips:

- Avoid unnecessarily long, drawn-out descriptions.
- Write short, well-structured sentences.
- Use short, linked paragraphs, with one or two main themes or issues in each.
- Use key terms wherever possible.
- Where appropriate, include a diagram and interpret it.
- Stick to the point of the question.
- Include examples you have come across in your own work – don't just rely on the coursebook.
- If the question is in two parts, make sure you can answer both parts.

The two examples below are the questions introduced in the previous section on interpreting diagrams. They show how you can use these diagrams to improve your responses to questions.

Example 1: *The government has embarked on an economic policy that is designed to provide a fiscal boost to reduce unemployment. Comment on whether this is likely to be successful.* **[12]**

The wording of the question invites you to consider both sides of an economic policy, indicating that an evaluation response is required here. Below is an appropriate structure for your answer.

Opening paragraph
- Define what is meant by fiscal policy and how it operates.
- Explain what is meant by fiscal boost and when it is usually used.

↓ link

Paragraph 2
- Analyse how a fiscal boost affects aggregate demand; use the diagram.

↓ link

Paragraph 3
- Analyse alternative ways in which a fiscal boost can be made.
- Explain their impact on the level of employment/unemployment.

↓ link

Paragraph 4
- Consider reasons why a fiscal boost might not be effective and therefore not successful in reducing unemployment.

link

Conclusion
- Building on the above, make very clear whether a fiscal boost is the best way for reducing unemployment in an economy.

Example 2: *Explain why in monopolistic competition there is an inefficient allocation of resources.* **[12]**

The command word in the question hints that you will need to employ a level of critical thinking and analysis in order to answer this question.

Below is an appropriate structure for your answer.

Opening paragraph
- Define monopolistic competition.
- Give a few examples of this market structure.
- Say how firms compete.

link

Paragraph 2
- Draw the short-run equilibrium diagram and interpret it.
- Say why there is an inefficient allocation of resources, referring to your diagram.

link

Paragraph 3
- Explain how abnormal profits will attract new firms into the industry.
- Explain how this will increase supply, resulting in a fall in demand, shifting the AC downwards until it is at the point where AR = AC (use the long-run diagram).

link

Paragraph 4
- Make clear why this again represents an inefficient allocation of resources due to excess capacity.
- Repeat how the firm operates above the minimum point of its AC curve in both short and long term.

Learning outcomes

The exercises in this chapter will help you to practise what you have learnt about:

■ the fundamental economic problem

■ scarcity and the inevitability of choices that have to be made by individuals, firms and governments

■ opportunity cost

■ why the basic questions of what, how and for whom production takes place have to be addressed in all economies

■ the meaning of the term 'ceteris paribus'

■ what is meant by the margin and decision-making at the margin

■ the importance of the time dimension in economics

■ the difference between positive and normative statements

■ what is meant by factors of production, namely land, labour, capital and enterprise and the role of enterprise in the modern economy

■ what is meant by the division of labour

■ how resources are allocated in market, planned and mixed economies

■ issues of transition when central planning in an economy is reduced

■ the characteristics of a production possibility curve and how opportunity cost can be applied

■ the functions and characteristics of money and types of money

■ how goods can be classified into free goods, private goods, public goods, merit goods and demerit goods

■ the problems associated with information failure.

KEY TERMS

You should **know and understand** what is meant by the following key terms. These terms are defined in Chapter 1 of the course book.

Resources	Long run	Reallocation of resources	Non-rival
Wants	Very long run	Factor mobility	Quasi-public good
Scarcity	Positive statement	Economic growth	Free rider
Choice	Normative statement	Capital consumption	Merit good
Fundamental economic problem	Specialisation	Investment	Demerit good
Factors of production	Market	Developing economy	Information failure
Land	Division of labour	Money	Paternalism
Labour	Economic structure	Near money	Moral hazard
Capital	Economic system	Liquidity	Adverse selection
Enterprise/ Entrepreneur	Market economy	Liabilities	
Production	Command/planned economy	Private goods	
Consumption	Mixed economy	Excludability	
Opportunity cost	Market mechanism	Rivalry	
Short run	Production possibility curve	Public good	
		Non-excludable	

REMEMBER
This first section of the syllabus contains a wide range of content, much of it of on-going value and use for the remaining sections of both the AS Level and the A Level courses.

Exercises

1 Consider the fundamental economic problem. Write a few sentences to describe how it affects:

 i you and your family

 ii the government of your country

 iii a manufacturing business.

2 The four factors of production are shown in the table below. Use the table to describe each and give examples from your country.

	Description	Examples from your own country
Land		
Labour		
Capital		
Enterprise		

3 Insert some words of your own in the gaps.

 Specialisation is where …… It can apply in the case of people in the workplace, for example …… A consequence of specialisation is that …… The division of labour is where …… It has important benefits for a firm and for the economy including ……

4 Economists refer to three main types of economy. For each, give an example country and say why you have chosen it. Then answer the question that follows.

 i Free market economy.

 ii Planned economy.

 iii Mixed economy.

 What problems have you experienced when making your choices?

5 Figure 1.1 shows a production possibility curve for an economy.

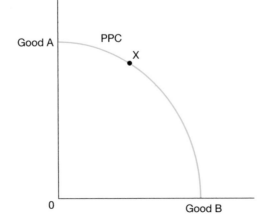

Figure 1.1 Production possibility curve for an economy

28

i Suppose the demand for good B increases. Insert a new point Y on the PPC to show how resources have been reallocated.

ii How does opportunity cost apply to the new position?

iii Suppose there is a general increase in unemployment in the economy. Insert a new point Z on the diagram and say what it means for the allocation of resources.

iv Draw a new PPC (PPC1), on the diagram to show how economic growth has affected the allocation of resources and say what this means.

v The production of good B has become more specialised. Draw a further PPC (PPC2) on the diagram to show how this has affected the allocation of resources and say what it means.

6 Opportunity cost is defined as the best alternative forgone. (Remember that it is measured in terms of a benefit and **not** in monetary terms).

Use a few examples to explain how:

i you and your family

ii your government

iii a manufacturing business

experiences opportunity cost in the decisions that each has to make.

7 The following are descriptions of the use of money:

A It allows prices to be easily established.

B Money has a value over time.

C Money is acceptable to buyers and sellers.

D Some household bills can be paid later.

Match the description with the functions of money in the table below and say how each is relevant in your country.

	Which one?	Relevance in your country
Medium of exchange		
Unit of account		
Standard of deferred payment		
Store of wealth		

8 The characteristics of public goods are non-excludability and non-rivalry. Give some examples of public goods from your own country and say why they match the stated characteristics. Use the table below.

Example	Comment
1	
2	
3	
4	

9 Merit goods are those goods and services that, due to information failure, will be under-consumed. This means that the benefit received from their consumption is greater than realised by the consumer. Complete the table below for your own country.

	Who provides and how?	Benefits
School education		
Local health care		

10 Demerit goods in contrast are over-provided due to information failure. Consumers are not fully aware of the effects of consuming these goods. Complete the table below for your own country.

	Costs	How does your government intervene?
Smoking		
Gambling		
Junk food and fizzy drinks		

Exam-style questions

Data response question

Difficult choices for the UK's National Health Service

The UK's National Health Service (NHS) is almost 70 years old. One of its core principles is that good healthcare and treatments should be available to all, irrespective of income or wealth. With the exception of prescriptions, optical and dental services charges, for which many people are exempt, the NHS in England is free at the point of use to all UK residents.

Funding for the NHS, like other areas of government spending, comes directly from taxation. For 2015/16, the overall NHS budget was £116.4 billion, a substantial part of central government spending on goods and services. The trend in the NHS budget from 2009/10, including planned expenditure to 2020/21, is shown in Figure 1.2.

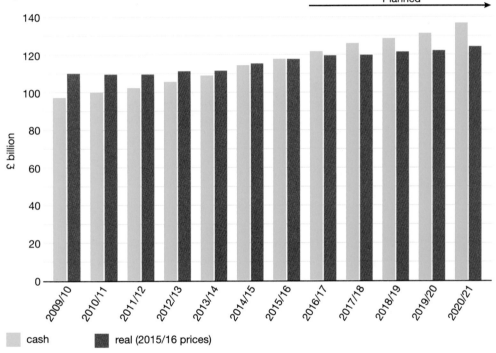

Figure 1.2 The NHS budget and how it has changed. NB: Real figures are at 2015/16 prices.

Source: Department of Health annual report and accounts 2014-15 and Spending Review end Autumn statement 2015.

The NHS budget is under ever-increasing pressures; people are living longer, some of new drugs that are prescribed are becoming more expensive and the number of people eligible for NHS treatment has increased.

It is hardly surprising, therefore, that there is growing support for the idea that some services, especially for those who can afford it, should be charged for rather than be free of charge. It seems almost inevitable that new charges will have to be introduced at some point in the future.

a With reference to Figure 1.2:

   i Describe the trend in the NHS budget from 2009/10 to 2015/16. **[2]**

   ii How does this differ from the projected trend from 2015/16 to 2020/21? **[2]**

   iii What is the difference between cash and real prices? **[2]**

31

b Apply the concept of opportunity cost to explain why the NHS is increasingly faced with having to make difficult choices. **[4]**

c Explain why NHS healthcare is a typical example of a merit good. **[4]**

d Discuss whether the NHS should charge at the point of use for some treatments that are currently free. **[6]**

> **TIP**
>
> You might find that you have to leave part **d** until you have rather more knowledge of economics. Why not try to answer the question and return to it later?

Essay questions

1 With reference to a production possibility curve (PPC), explain the difference between a movement along a PPC and a shift outwards of a PPC. **[8]**

> **TIP**
>
> Be careful to label the axes on the PPC correctly. They must refer to two different types of good e.g. consumer goods and capital goods or Good A and Good B.

2 Using examples from your own country, explain the role of enterprise in an economy. **[8]**

3 Explain why public goods and merit goods cannot be fully provided in a market economy. **[8]**

4 Explain the difference between the characteristics of money and its functions in a modern economy. **[8]**

5 With the aid of examples, show how opportunity cost applies to consumers, producers and the government of an economy. **[8]**

Multiple choice questions

1 As an economics student, you decide to revise for your examination rather than play with your friends in a cricket team. What is the opportunity cost of your decision?

  A You might get a higher mark in the examination.

  B Your cricket team lose the match.

  C The enjoyment you would get if you had played in the match.

  D The money you have saved by staying at home.

2 Figure 1.3 shows the production possibilities for an economy.

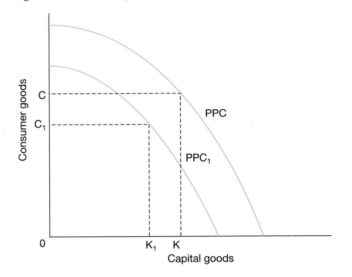

Figure 1.3

The production possibility curve (PPC) has changed from PPC to PPC_1 due to:

A An increase in unemployment.

B The exhaustion of a valuable natural resource.

C An increase in the capital stock of the economy.

D Less spending on consumer goods.

3 Which of these is **not** a normative statement?

   A The rate of inflation in Pakistan in 2016 was 4.8%.

   B The rate of inflation in Pakistan in 2016 was reasonable.

   C Inflation in Pakistan in 2016 should affect the poor more than the rich.

   D The rate of inflation in Pakistan in 2016 may have led to the depreciation of the rupee.

4 Figure 1.4 shows the production possibilities for a garment manufacture.

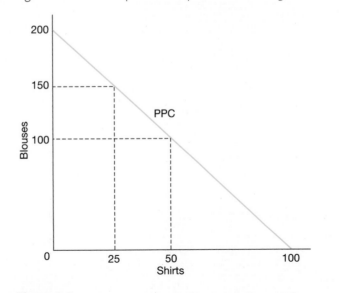

Figure 1.4

The garment manufacturer has received an urgent order requiring an increase in the production of shirts from 25 to 50 units.

What is the opportunity cost?

A 25 units of shirts.

B 50 units of shirts.

C 100 units of blouses.

D 50 units of blouses.

5 Which of these is an example of a public good?

   A State education that is free to students.

   B Public libraries.

   C A public health service.

   D The local police force.

Learning outcomes

The exercises in this chapter will help you to practise what you have learnt about:

- what a market is and what effective demand in a market is
- what is meant by demand and supply
- what is meant by individual and market demand and supply and how demand and supply curves can be derived
- which factors influence demand and supply
- the meaning of elasticity
- price, income and cross elasticity of demand – what each means, how they are calculated, what factors affect them and the implications for revenue and business decisions
- price elasticity of supply – what it means, how it is calculated, the factors affecting it and the implications of how businesses react to changed market conditions
- what is meant by equilibrium and disequilibrium in a market
- how the interaction of demand and supply leads to equilibrium in a market
- how changes in demand and supply affect the equilibrium price and quantity and how this analysis can be applied
- the difference between movements along and shifts of demand and supply curves
- the meaning of joint demand and joint supply
- how the price mechanism works with respect to rationing, signalling and the transmission of preferences
- what is meant by consumer surplus and producer surplus and their significance
- how these are affected by changes in equilibrium price and quantity.

KEY TERMS

You should **know and understand** what is meant by the following key terms. These terms are defined in Chapter 2 of the course book.

Price mechanism	Supply	Price elasticity of supply
Market	Supply curve	Equilibrium
Demand	Supply schedule	Equilibrium price
Notional demand	Subsidy	Equilibrium quantity
Effective demand	Elasticity	Disequilibrium
Demand curve	Elastic	Change in demand
Market demand	Inelastic	Specific tax
Demand schedule	Price elasticity of demand	*Ad valorem* tax
Normal goods	Perfectly inelastic	Joint supply
Inferior goods	Perfectly elastic	Transmission of preferences
Substitute	Unit elasticity	Consumer surplus
Complement	Income elasticity of demand	Producer surplus
Joint demand	Cross elasticity of demand	

REMEMBER

The content of this chapter is very important in the AS microeconomic syllabus; it also underpins much of the A Level syllabus.

Exercises

1 The table below shows the market demand for rail travel between two cities in India.

Price (Rupees)	No. of trips per day ('000)
4,000	20
3,500	22
3,000	25
2,500	30
2,000	35
1,500	43
1,000	50

Table 2.1

i Use the data to construct a demand curve.

ii If the price of rail travel was 2,400 rupees, what would be the quantity demanded?

iii On your diagram:

– Show how the demand curve changes if there is an increase in disposable income.

– Show how the demand curve changes if a new express bus service undercuts the rail fare.

2

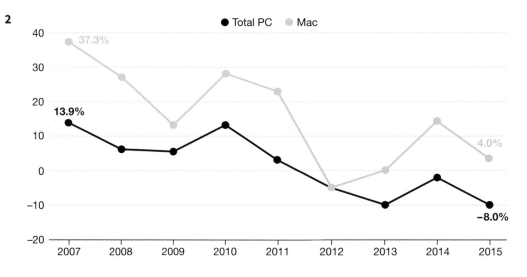

Figure 2.1 The PC's misery hasn't affected Apple

i Compare the change in the sales of Apple Mac computers with that of all PC manufacturers.

ii Apply the determinants of demand to explain the changes that you have identified.

3 Price elasticity of demand (PED) measures the responsiveness of the quantity demanded for a product in relation to a change in its price.

Make a note of the formula and then complete the table below.

PED	Numerical values	Typical products	Effect on total revenue when price changes
Price elastic			
Price inelastic			

4 Income elasticity of demand is a numerical measure of the responsiveness of the quantity demanded for a product following a change in income.

Make a note of the formula and then complete the table below.

Type of good	Numerical value	Typical products	What happens when income changes
Normal good			
Inferior good			

5 Cross elasticity of demand measures how the quantity demanded for one product responds to a change in the price of another related product. Make a note of the formula and then complete the table below:

Type of product	Sign and size	Typical examples	Use of cross elasticity to a business
Substitutes			
Complements			

6 A manufacturer of solar water pumps in Kenya believes that the business can respond quickly to price changes in the market. At a price of $1,000 the business is willing to supply 200 units. When the price suddenly increases to $1,250, the business clears all of its stock and now supplies 220 units.

i Calculate the price elasticity of supply.

ii Is the Kenyan manufacturer correct in believing that his business 'can respond quickly to price changes in the market'?

iii The Kenyan manufacturer's main competitor is a German business. At a price of $1,000, this firm was also willing to supply 200 units; at the increased price of $1,250, it was able to supply 260 units. What might you conclude from this? Is there anything that the Kenyan manufacturer might do to become more competitive?

7 Figure 2.2 shows a market equilibrium position.

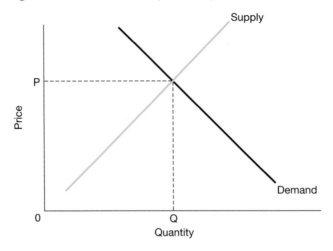

Figure 2.2 Market equilibrium position

i On Figure 2.2:

- Show how the equilibrium position changes when consumer income falls.

- Show how the equilibrium position changes when there is a reduction in supply.

- Identify the new equilibrium position when there is a fall in consumer income with a simultaneous reduction in supply.

ii Write a few notes to explain what determines the change in the equilibrium position in each of the above cases.

8 Research for a new Indonesian food producer estimated that the price of elasticity of demand for its ready-made Sambal sauce is 1.25 and 0.9 during holiday periods.

i Say what these estimates mean. **[Ap]**

ii Explain why the estimates differ. **[A]**

iii Discuss the extent to which price alone might determine the demand for this product. **[E]**

9 It has been reported that the thirst for high quality Arabica coffee has meant that production was not keeping up with increasing global demand (*Daily Telegraph*, 4 January 2016).

i Use a diagram to show how this is likely to affect the market for Arabica coffee. **[Ap]**

ii Analyse the possible causes of an increase in the demand for high quality Arabica coffee. **[A]**

iii Arabica coffee prices have fallen despite the increase in demand. Discuss why this has occurred and the effects on Arabica coffee producers. **[E]**

10 i Explain the difference between consumer surplus and producer surplus. **[Ap]**

ii Using diagrams, analyse what happens to consumer surplus and to producer surplus when the price of a good increases. **[A]**

iii Discuss the ways in which consumers might maximise their consumer surplus and producers might maximise their producer surplus. **[E]**

REMEMBER
Price elasticity of demand is an estimate due to the way in which the data is collected at two different periods of time.

TIP
There are other lower quality types of coffee produced especially by growers in South East Asia.

Exam-style questions

Data response question

Cocoa crop hit by worst Saharan storm in two decades

The price of chocolate bars is set to soar following the devastating effects of the latest Harmattan dust storm to hit cocoa plantations in West Africa. Production in Ghana and the Ivory Coast has been worst affected; the dust storm dries out the soil and slows the growth of the precious cocoa pods. Production in the Ivory Coast is 12% down on the previous harvest; prices have risen by as much as 52% in response to the adverse weather.

All of this is bad news for consumers and chocolate manufacturers. Or is it? The global demand for chocolate, particularly that with 70% cocoa, is increasing. This increase in demand is particularly noticeable in the emerging BRIC economies where more and more middle class consumers are purchasing chocolate bars from the big multinational producers like Nestlé and Hershey. Elsewhere, in the UK for example, the demand for chocolate is falling but for different reasons mainly connected to pressures to reduce the sugar content of the diets of young people especially.

Cocoa traders expect the imbalance between supply and demand to persist – a 30% rise in cocoa prices is expected over the next five years. Whether this will actually happen is not entirely dependent on market forces given that the crops of cocoa producers are subject to perennial problems of bad weather and pests.

Source: Bloomberg Business, 19 January 2016 (adapted).

39

a Describe how the world price of cocoa beans is determined. **[2]**

b Use a diagram to explain how the fall in supply has affected the market for cocoa beans. **[4]**

c Explain the likely effects of adverse weather for cocoa farmers in the Ivory Coast. **[4]**

d Using the information provided, explain **one** reason why:

   i   The demand for chocolate in the BRIC countries is increasing.

   ii The demand for chocolate in the UK is falling. **[4]**

e Discuss the factors that will determine whether the forecast of a 30% rise in cocoa prices over the next five years will actually happen. **[6]**

Essay questions

1 **a** Explain what is meant by 'price elasticity of demand' and using examples, describe why the demand for some goods is price inelastic. **[8]**

   b Discuss how entrepreneurs might be able to make a good more price inelastic. Why might they be happier to change the price of a good that is price inelastic rather than one that is price elastic. **[12]**

2 a Explain two factors that are likely to make the supply of a product relatively price inelastic. **[8]**

b Discuss the policies that governments might use to increase the price elasticity of supply of essential goods, and assess the likely effectiveness of such policies. **[12]**

Cambridge International AS and A Level, 9708, Paper 22, Q3 February/March 2016.

3 a Explain how the concepts of income elasticity of demand and cross elasticity of demand can be applied to determine particular types of good. **[8]**

b Discuss how knowledge of these concepts might be useful to a car manufacturer in an emerging economy such as China or India. **[12]**

4 A recent television programme in the UK revealed that fresh and ground turmeric was a new 'super food' that could help offset a wide range of medical problems.

a Using diagrams, analyse how this revelation is likely to have affected the market for fresh and ground turmeric. **[8]**

b Discuss how and to what extent the market might be able to respond to this revelation. **[12]**

Multiple choice questions

1 Which of these situations is most likely to have resulted in a shift to the right in the demand curve for lap top computers?

A An increase in demand for personal computers.

B An increase in disposable incomes.

C A fall in the price of lap top computers.

D The launch of new model of mobile phone.

2 An Indonesian airline typically sells 5,000 tickets per month for travel to Australia at an average price of $600. When it reduces the price to $540, it sells 6,000 tickets per month. Which of these is true for the price elasticity of demand and change in revenue?

	Price elasticity of demand	Change in revenue
A	–2	increase
B	–2	decrease
C	–0.5	increase
D	–0.5	decrease

3 The income elasticity of demand for designer jeans is estimated at + 1.6. Which of the following is most correct?

A As income rises, the price of designer jeans increased by 60%.

B An increase in income of 10% will result in no change in the demand for designer jeans.

C Consumers will switch from buying cheaper jeans to buying designer jeans.

D Designer jeans are a normal good meaning that an increase in income will lead to an increase in demand.

4 Imagine the demand curve for a product with unitary price elasticity of demand. Which of the following is true?

   A A fall in price will lead to an increase in total expenditure.

   B A fall in price will lead to a fall in total expenditure.

   C As price increases, total expenditure remains the same.

   D As price increases, total expenditure increases.

5 A clothing manufacturer receives an urgent order to increase the supply of garments from the factory. Which of the following will be of greatest help enabling the manufacturer to fulfil this request?

   A Unemployed workers are available.

   B The garments can be processed in a few weeks.

   C The factory has spare capacity.

   D New machinery can easily be purchased.

Think like an economist

Key economic myth

It is a myth that markets operate in the way that economic theory says they should work. The twin forces of demand and supply do exert some control over markets but it is rare to find a market that has been unaffected by factors other than demand and supply. Increasingly, where this occurs, it leads to market failure and an inefficient allocation of resources.

Key economist

The obvious choice of economist for this chapter is **Adam Smith**. As a political economist writing at the end of the 18th century, he is best known in microeconomics for the term 'invisible hand'. He referred to this as the unobservable market force that helps the demand and supply of goods in a free market to automatically reach equilibrium.

In a free market, there are no restrictions and regulations imposed on sellers and buyers by the government. For example, if a producer lowers his price, customers will buy more. It follows that other producers will have to do likewise or offer a better product otherwise they will lose business. Smith also championed the view that when customers demand something, someone will supply it. There will be equilibrium since customers are happy and producers get the price they desire.

Key economic issue

A key economic issue in many markets is how long it takes for the market to respond to changes in demand and supply. Simple economic theory invariably assumes 'immediately'; the reality is that changes in demand, as well as changes in supply, do invariably take time before they affect the market. In some cases, it can be a matter of years, in others just a few minutes. Knowing this is necessary when businesses are considering how to respond to changing market conditions.

Key economic policy

In most markets, there is intense competition between producers of similar goods. Carbonated drinks (soda) and branded fast food are typical examples of competitive markets that are increasingly global. A key policy is what price should be charged and what might happen if price changes.

It might seem an easy decision, given the economic concepts in this chapter but it isn't. Producers have to anticipate how their competitors will react to a price change. They must also be mindful of their own price elasticity of demand (if they know it) and whether that of their competitors' is different.

As a general rule:

- if the price elasticity of demand is price inelastic, then a price increase will increase revenue from sales
- if the price elasticity of demand is price elastic, a reduction in price will increase revenue from sales.

The other two possibilities should not be pursued. Just how long the above rules hold true is difficult to predict since it will depend on how competitors react to these price changes.

Improve your answer

Read the question and answer below and see how you can improve it using the suggestions that follow.

Question

a *Explain the difference between a movement along a demand curve and a shift of a demand curve. [8]*

b *Suppose there is an increase in demand for a product. Comment upon the factors that are likely to determine the new market equilibrium. [12]*

a The demand for a product depends upon various factors such as price as well as consumers' income. A demand curve shows the relationship between demand and the price of a product. Most demand curves slope downwards showing that when price falls more is demanded.

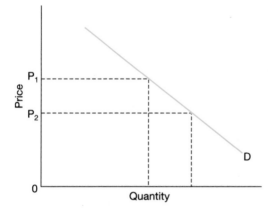

A movement along a demand curve is due to a change in price, up or down, whereas a shift in the demand curve is due to other factors such as income.

b An increase in demand can be caused by various things such as an increase in income on the part of consumers. As previously mentioned, this results in a shift to the right of the individual's demand curve. This leads to an increase in price as well as an increase in the quantity demanded.

43

The extent of the increase in demand is more difficult to assess. It depends on various things like how big has been the shift of the demand curve and the slope of the supply curve. The diagram below shows some of the possibilities.

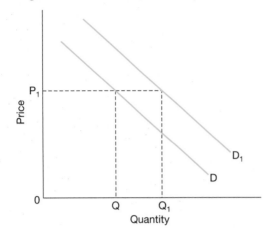

Suggestions on how to improve your answer

Part a

This answer is very brief, too brief in fact. The first diagram is incomplete. Additional labels need to be inserted to show what is meant by a movement along a demand curve. Labels are missing on the horizontal axis.

The explanation of a movement along a demand curve can then follow, referring to the diagram. Much more is needed to explain the factors that can lead to a shift, outwards and inwards, of a demand curve. You should refer to a change in income, changes in the prices of substitutes and complements and taste factors. Suggest another two paragraphs.

Part b

Another very weak response. The second diagram is incomplete since it does not include a supply curve (the question states a new market equilibrium). You could also add a further diagram that shows what happens when demand is more price elastic.

Reference to the size of the shift is ok but needs elaboration. The new market equilibrium though is determined by the slope of the demand curve, not the supply curve.

Learning outcomes

The exercises in this chapter will help you to practise what you have learnt about:

- why governments may find it necessary to intervene in the workings of the price mechanism
- how maximum and minimum prices work and their effect on the market
- why governments impose taxes
- the difference between direct and indirect taxes and how to analyse their impact and incidence
- what is meant by specific and *ad valorem* taxes
- the difference between average and marginal rates of taxation
- the meaning of proportional, progressive and regressive taxes
- what is meant by the 'Canons of taxation'
- how subsidies impact on the market and their incidence
- what is meant by transfer payments and how to analyse their effect on the market
- why governments directly provide goods and services and their effect on the market
- what is meant by nationalisation and privatisation and how to assess their effect on the market.

KEY TERMS

You should **know and understand** what is meant by the following key terms. These terms are defined in Chapter 3 of the course book.

Market failure	**Incidence**
Regulation	**Proportional tax**
Taxes	**Progressive tax**
Maximum price	**Regressive tax**
Minimum price	**Transfer payment**
Canon of taxation	**Nationalisation**
Direct tax	**Privatisation**
Indirect tax	

Exercises

1   Maximum and minimum prices interfere with the normal workings of the market mechanism.
    Complete the table below to show their differences.

	Above or below equilibrium price?	Effect on market	Where used
Maximum price			
Minimum price			

2   Malaysia, like most economies, has a typical taxation structure, some details of which are shown below. An important distinction is between direct and indirect taxes and whether the taxes are progressive or regressive. See if you can complete the table below.

	Direct or Indirect?	Progressive or Regressive?	Likely purpose
Income tax			
Goods & services tax (GST)			
Excise duties on tobacco and mah-jong tiles			
Real property gains tax			
Import duties			
Corporate taxes			

3   The incidence of a tax is the extent to which the burden is borne by the producer, the consumer or both.

Complete each of the diagrams in Figure 3.1 to show the incidence of imposing an indirect *ad valorem* tax on a good. Make a few notes on any differences you observe.

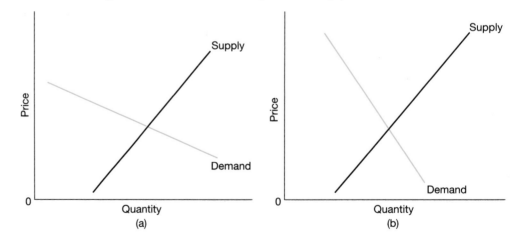

Figure 3.1 Incidence of imposing an indirect *ad valorem* tax on a good

4   A subsidy is a payment that is made to suppliers in order to reduce their costs and encourage them to increase output. Think about your own country and what subsidies are paid. Then complete the table below:

Type of subsidy	Advantages of subsidy	Disadvantages of subsidy

5   Insert a few words to complete the phrases in the paragraphs below.

   i   A transfer payment is one that …… An example from my country is …… The purpose of this payment is …… It affects the market through ……

   ii   The direct provision of goods and services is used by governments in order to …… In my country, such provision includes …… It may not be the most effective way of provision because ……

6   The government of Kenya has set monthly maximum wholesale and retail prices for petrol since 2010. The following year, it set a maximum price for sugar.

   i   Give some likely reasons for each of these controls. **[Ap]**

   ii   Using diagrams, compare the likely effects of maximum prices on the markets for petrol and sugar in Kenya. **[A]**

   iii   Comment on the view that the 'Kenyan government is misguided in its application of maximum price controls – these markets would be much better served if prices were left to the free market'. **[E]**

TIP
You will probably need to have studied the next section of the syllabus before you can answer part (iii).

7   Iran is the world's biggest producer of pistachio nuts and also produces 90% of the world's saffron. Both products are heavily subsidised by the Iranian government.

   i   Give some reasons for these subsidies. **[Ap]**

   ii   Use a diagram to show how the subsidies paid by the Iranian government affect the world market for pistachio nuts. **[A]**

   iii   Discuss why the subsidies paid by the Iranian government to its farmers might conflict with the practices advocated by the World Trade Organization (WTO). **[E]**

8   Pakistan has undertaken a massive programme of privatisation of its manufacturing, banking, oil and gas and transport industries over the past 20 years. The programme is continuing.

   Assess some of the likely benefits and costs of these privatisations for the Pakistan economy and its people. **[E]**

REMEMBER
You do not need to know anything about Pakistan, only that it is a lower-income economy.

47

Exam-style questions

Data response question

Pakistan's case for agricultural subsidies

Prior to the 2015–2016 federal budget, the Ministry of National Food Security in Pakistan made a strong case to the Ministry of Finance for a subsidy to be paid to the country's struggling farmers. Extreme weather, floods and droughts have resulted in poor crops of cotton, rice and wheat, which have affected their incomes. The proposed subsidy would be paid on agricultural inputs such as seeds, fertilisers and pesticides to reduce the cost of production for farmers.

The case put forward referred to the high prices of these farm inputs which in turn led to high food prices. A subsidy through a reduction in the wheat support price rather than on agricultural inputs would benefit low income families and increase exports at a time when India and Bangladesh were providing heavy subsidies to their own farmers.

Around the same time, at the World Trade Organization, the Pakistan government has demanded that rich and large developing countries should eliminate export and production subsidies on crops such as cotton, sugar and wheat. A government minister stressed that 'Cotton is the economic lifeline of Pakistan. Once subsidies are removed, the entire increase in the value of cotton would be reflected in the textile and clothing sectors'.

Source: The Express Tribune, 19 December 2015 and budget.par.com.pk

a Describe how opportunity cost applies to the Ministry of Finance's decision on whether to increase agricultural subsides. **[2]**

b Using a diagram, analyse how a subsidy to Pakistan's wheat farmers will affect the market for wheat. **[4]**

c Explain how the proposed subsidy is likely to affect Pakistan's external economy. **[4]**

d Consider how, apart from subsidies, Pakistan's poorest farmers might be supported. **[4]**

e Comment on whether agricultural subsidies should only be paid to producers in lower-income economies like Pakistan. **[6]**

Essay questions

1 Discuss why it is often necessary for governments to provide goods and services. **[12]**

2 In September 2016, the Indian government cut the import tax on wheat from 25% to 10%; the import tax on refined palm oil fell from 20% to 15%.

Using diagrams, compare the effects on the markets for these products. **[12]**

3 The UK is to tax the sugar used in fizzy drinks (soda) on the grounds that this will help to reduce a growing problem of obesity in children and young adults.

Discuss whether this new increase is likely to achieve its objective. **[12]**

> **TIP**
> A two-sided answer is required, ideally with a relevant final judgement.

Multiple choice questions

1 Figure 3.2 hows the effects of placing an indirect tax equal to AD on a product.

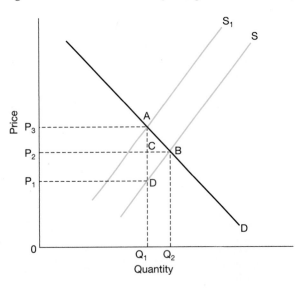

Figure 3.2

Which of the areas below represents the burden of the tax on consumers of the product?

A P_2BDP_1 **B** P_3ACP_2 **C** P_3ABP_2 **D** P_2CDP_1

2 Which of the following transfer payments is likely to be the best way of providing a more equitable distribution of income?

   A An increase in the monthly allowance for old people.

   B An increase in maternity payments.

   C Introduction of free travel on buses.

   D More information is required before a decision can be made.

3 Figure 3.3 shows the demand and supply of wheat over a four-year period. The initial equilibrium is at E. Supply in subsequent years is S_1 to S_4.

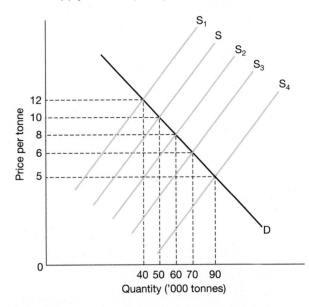

Figure 3.3

49

The government's agricultural policy is to maintain the income of wheat farmers at the initial equilibrium level. To achieve this, in which year will the government have to provide the most subsidy?

A Year 1.   **B** Year 2.   **C** Year 3.   **D** Year 4.

4 A government badly needs a new motorway link to its international airport and has determined that this link should be privately funded.

Which is the strongest likely reason for this privatisation?

A A new motorway link is essential to meet the needs of airport passengers.

B A new motorway link will reduce congestion.

C The government does not have sufficient capital to fund it.

D Employees will be able to buy shares in the new company.

5 The table below shows for minimum price control and for maximum price control where prices should be fixed in relation to the equilibrium price. Which is correct?

	Minimum price control	Maximum price control
A	above	below
B	above	above
C	below	below
D	below	above

Think like an economist

Key economic myth

Maximum and minimum prices always provide a more effective allocation of resources in the market than if the market is left to the free market forces of demand and supply.

Markets are not allocating resources effectively if prices are too high. If we are dealing with essential food items such as bread and rice or public housing, then there appears to be a strong argument for the government to intervene in order to assist poor families. Imposing a maximum price makes products more affordable; however, economic theory indicates that supply will fall due to lower prices. Some consumers are now going to be worse off due to shortages. Long queues for food are likely to occur and even worse, some supplies will be diverted to informal, hidden markets.

Imposing a minimum price is also well-intentioned but leads to a problem of over-supply. Minimum prices tend to be set for goods with negative externalities such as cigarettes or for essential food items in order to give producers an incentive to supply the market. With demerit goods, a high minimum price invariably leads to supplies feeding the informal market; for essential food items, there is likely to be excess supply in the market.

Key economist

Paul Samuelson has contributed to many branches of economics. His textbook, *Economics*, was first produced in 1948 and has been updated on regular basis since then. It is without doubt a milestone in the development of economics as a scientific study.

Samuelson is probably best known for introducing the concept of 'revealed preference'. Like much of his pioneering work, he observed whether consumers were better off after a change in prices and how this could be measured. He was also the first economist to define the characteristics of public goods, based on the assumption that the market could not provide because of the problems of charging those who benefited from them.

Key diagrams

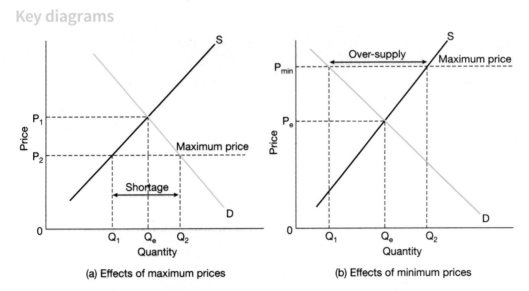

(a) Effects of maximum prices

(b) Effects of minimum prices

Figure 3.4 Effects of maximum and minimum prices

Key points to note are:

a To be effective, the maximum price must always be fixed below the free market equilibrium. A price set above P max will have no effect on the market.

b To be effective, the minimum price must always be fixed above the free market equilibrium. A price set below P min will have no effect on the market.

Key economic issue

The key economic issue is whether maximum or minimum price control is the best way of combatting market failure in particular markets. There are opportunity cost considerations as in any situation where government spending is taking place. There is also the issue of how best to pay the subsidy – should it be direct to farmers or should it be to keep market prices at a maximum level? Other forms of government intervention such as subsidies, indirect taxation, transfer payments and state/direct provision of merit and public goods should also be considered.

Key economic policy

High food and fuel prices have been a major economic and political issue in Kenya. The practice of price controls was abandoned in the mid-1990s and replaced by a policy of letting the market determine prices through the usual forces of demand and supply. In 2011, after much debate, price controls on essential goods such a maize, rice, wheat, sugar, cooking oil, petrol, diesel and paraffin were introduced in an attempt to put a brake on price rises which were increasing at a faster rate than incomes.

The Consumer Federation of Kenya was against price controls, arguing that it would lead to the hoarding of commodities in the market. Manufacturers were also against, claiming that consumer prices would become and remain lower than controlled prices if controls were removed. Farmers claimed that output levels would fall and less attention would be paid to productivity.

The key question is: 'Are price controls the answer to Kenya's problem of high food prices?' The short answer is 'probably not'. This is because price controls may have certain merits when markets are not working properly but as a long-term measure, they have not worked in the past for Kenya or elsewhere.

Improve your answer

Read the question and answer below and see how you can improve it using the suggestions that follow.

Question

a *Explain the impact on the market of a subsidy paid to wheat producers. [8]*

b *Comment on the view of the Asian Development Bank that 'Targeted food subsidies would help South Asia cope with future food price spikes'. [12]*

a A subsidy is a payment made directly to a producer, in this case, the wheat farmer. The payments come direct from the government or in the case of Europe, the European Commission through its controversial Common Agricultural Policy. Subsidies are paid to agricultural producers in developed as well as in emerging and developing economies. Their impact on the market is shown on the diagram below.

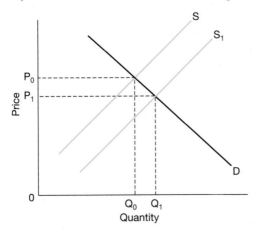

Figure 3.5 The impact of a subsidy on the market

Without government intervention, the market price is higher and the output is lower compared to when a subsidy is paid to wheat farmers. The effect of the subsidy is to lower price and increase the amount of wheat that is produced. The subsidy reduces the cost of producing wheat as far as farmers are concerned; consumers of wheat also benefit.

b The rocketing price of food is a big problem for poor families. In India, for example, the price of wheat and rice has increased by around 20% in the last year. The same is also true for Pakistan and for Bangladesh. The poorest families are being badly affected since the increases are on their staple food items and they have no surplus income to pay for the price increases. People in Sri Lanka are also vulnerable since they import all the wheat they consume.

The reasons for the price rise are relevant. The last two years have been blighted by poor weather which has reduced supply in wheat growing areas. The rice crop has also been affected. The population of many countries in South Asia continues to increase yet the output of staple foods does not appear to have increased that much. It is also relevant that India has recently restricted its exports of rice.

The Asian Development Bank is right when it says that subsidies will keep down future price rises of food items. This follows from what was explained in part (a). Subsidies are therefore a good way of helping those in most need.

Food subsidies are not without problems, though. The problem is that once applied, they are difficult to remove as when this happens, prices will shoot back to where they were or above the price level before subsidisation. There is also an element of opportunity cost. The government has to consider whether the money it spends on food subsidies could be more effectively spent on something else like primary education or food vouchers for those most in need. Another consideration is whether with subsidised crops, farmers will not try to be more efficient in the way in which they produce their crops. There is little incentive to innovate.

To conclude, as shown above, the Asian Development Bank is right but only to a certain extent. Subsidies can help to reduce future food prices but only if they are carefully managed in relation to future market conditions.

Suggestions on how to improve this answer

Overall, as it has been written, this is a very good answer that in both parts, focuses on the point of the question. Part **(b)** is particularly good as the student is successful in setting out the context (no doubt largely from own knowledge). This is to be encouraged.

Minor suggestions are:

Part a More explicit use could be made of the diagram. This would give more meaning to the second paragraph. Reference might be made to how the subsidy might be paid.

Part b There is not really much that can be added to this answer; there is a clear conclusion with some final judgement. Excellent given the time constraint. The first two paragraphs have some valid context, which is helpful. The last three paragraphs are clearly evaluative, with a judgement in the last paragraph. It is good to see non-textbook knowledge.

2.4 The macroeconomy (AS Level)

Learning outcomes

The exercises in this chapter will help you to practise what you have learnt about:

- the determinants of aggregate demand and aggregate supply and understanding the shapes of their curves
- how changes in the price level are measured and the difference between money values and real values
- the causes and consequences of inflation, deflation and disinflation
- the components of the balance of payments
- the distinction between a balance of payments equilibrium and disequilibrium
- the causes and consequences of balance of payments disequilibrium
- different types of exchange rate
- the determination of different exchange rates in different exchange rate systems
- the causes and consequences of exchange rate changes
- what is meant by the terms of trade and how they can be estimated
- the causes and consequences of changes in the terms of trade
- the distinction between absolute and comparative advantage
- the benefits of free trade
- the main characteristics of free trade areas, customs unions and economic unions
- the methods of and arguments in favour of protectionism.

55

KEY TERMS

You should **know and understand** what is meant by the following key terms. These terms are defined in Chapter 4 of the course book.

Macroeconomy	Demand-pull inflation	Floating exchange rate	Free trade area
Aggregate demand	Monetarists	Fixed exchange rate	Customs union
Aggregate supply	Menu costs	Hot money flows	Economic union
Short-run aggregate supply	Shoe-leather costs	Managed float	Trade creation
	Fiscal drag	Depreciation	Trade diversion
Long-run aggregate supply	Inflationary noise	Devaluation	Protectionism
	Deflation	Marshall–Lerner condition	Tariff
Keynesians	Disinflation		Quota
New classical economists	Balance of payments	J-curve effect	Exchange control
	Current account	Appreciation	Embargo
Macroeconomic equilibrium	Capital account	Revaluation	Voluntary export restraint
	Financial account	Terms of trade	
Inflation	Net errors and omissions	Absolute advantage	Infant industries
Creeping inflation		Comparative advantage	Dumping
Hyperinflation	Exchange rate		
Consumer price index	Trade weighted exchange rate	Free trade	
Money values		Trading possibility curve	
Real values	Real effective exchange rate		
Cost-push inflation		Trade bloc	

Exercises

1 Aggregate demand is the total spending on goods and services in an economy at a given price level. Aggregate supply is the total output that is produced at a given price level.

Complete the table below for the short- and long-run time periods.

	Causes of short-run change	Causes of long-run shift
Aggregate demand		
Aggregate supply		

2 i In 2015 business confidence in Brazil increased in anticipation of the benefits to be gained from the 2016 Olympic Games. Show how this can be represented on an AD/AS diagram.

ii Also in 2015, the unemployment rate in Brazil increased to over 10%. Show how this can be represented on an AD/AS diagram.

iii Combine your two AD/AS diagrams and write a few sentences to explain their combined effect on the Brazilian economy in 2015.

3 The data below is for the economy of Namibia in 2014.

Total expenditure by category	US$m
Household final consumption	7,918
Capital formation	4,566*
Government final consumption	3,107
Exports	5,271
Imports	8,225

*estimate   *Source:* World Bank.

i Calculate the level of aggregate demand in 2014.

ii The government is developing a major new port facility at Walvis Bay. In which of the above categories would this expenditure be placed?

iii How might a depreciation of Namibia's exchange rate affect each of the categories of expenditure?

4 The charts in Figure 4.1 show the changes in consumer prices and the purchasing power of the Namibian dollar from 2003 to 2013.

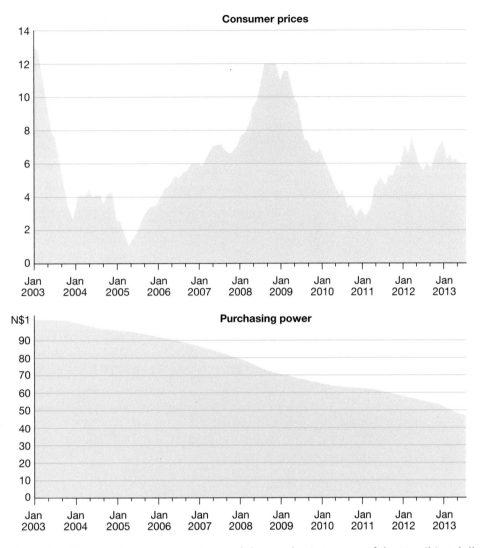

Figure 4.1 Changes in consumer prices and the purchasing power of the Namibian dollar from 2003–2013

i Describe the pattern of inflation in Namibia from 2003 to 2013.

ii Explain why the government of Namibia should be concerned about what is shown in the data.

5 The data below are for the current account of the balance of payments of Namibia in 2015.

	N$ million
Exports of goods	51,938
Imports of goods	89,131
Net trade in services (inc. transport & travel)	−1,132
Investment income (net)*	−631
Current transfers in cash and kind (net)**	18,792

*Now known as net primary income.
**Now known as net secondary income.

Source: Bank of Namibia.

57

i Calculate the balance of trade in goods and services.

ii Calculate the current account balance.

iii Why might the government of Namibia be concerned about its current account situation? What might it do to improve its position?

iv Obtain the same data for your own country and then repeat tasks (i)–(iii) above.

6 Figure 4.2 shows the exchange rate of the US dollar and the Brazilian real from 2012 to 2016.

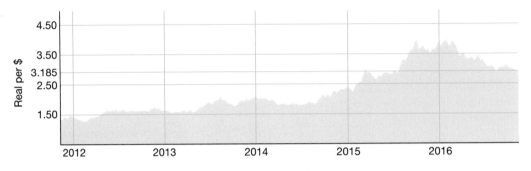

Figure 4.2 Exchange rate of the US dollar and the Brazilian real from 2012–2016

i Has the real appreciated or depreciated over this period?

ii Consider the data for 2016 when the Olympic Games were held in Brazil. How might the change in the exchange rate have affected international visitors to the Games?

7 Terms of trade is a numerical measure of the relationship between export and import prices.

Table 4.1 shows the terms of trade for Australia and for China from January 2014 to July 2016.

	Australia	China
January 2014	98.3	101.4
July 2014	92.7	100.0
January 2015	88.3	110.8
July 2015	82.6	111.9
January 2016	80.6	108.0
July 2016	80.5	101.4

Table 4.1 Terms of trade for Australia and China

i Compare the changes in the terms of trade for Australia and China from January 2014 to July 2016. Write a few sentences on what the changes mean for each economy.

ii Obtain similar data for the changes in the terms of trade for your country over the same period. Comment on what you have found out.

8 In the March Union Budget 2016, the Indian Finance Minister announced a major financial boost for farmers adversely affected by drought conditions. Additional funds were also allocated for expanding higher education.

    i Use an AD/AS diagram to explain the effects of these measures on the Indian economy. **[A]**

    ii Comment upon the criteria that might be used to assess if these measures have been effective. **[E]**

9 Consider the data presented in Table 4.2.

Brazil	Russia	India	China	S. Africa
6.2%	6.8%	10.9%	2.6%	6.8%

Table 4.2 Estimated annual rates of inflation of BRICs economies in 2014

    a Suggest why the rates of inflation in 2014 might have differed. **[A]**

    b India and China are trading competitors in some markets. Discuss how the differing rates of inflation might have affected their relative competitiveness. **[E]**

10 a Analyse why a developed economy might wish to protect a domestic industry and say which measures might be most appropriate. **[A]**

    b Comment on Paul Krugman's view that if economists shared a doctrine, it would surely include advocating free trade. **[E]**

Exam-style questions

Data response

Will universal free trade benefit the UK economy post-Brexit?

Prior to the referendum on EU membership (23 June 2016), 168 professional economists believed that Brexit would hurt the economy. From a trade perspective, they believed that 'dropping our tariffs would give up all of our negotiating power allowing other countries to raise tariffs and decimate our exporters' (Economists for Remain, *Daily Telegraph*, 21 June 2016).

This view was not one shared by Prof. Patrick Minford, a long-standing critic of the EU. He strongly advocated that with free trade agreements with countries around the world, these countries would lower their tariffs and trade barriers against the UK. In turn, the UK government would do likewise on trade with countries such as India, Canada, Australia, New Zealand, Singapore and even China.

Reducing protectionism in this way has many benefits for consumers – they will pay around 20% less for food and manufactured goods and therefore experience a fall in their cost of living. On the other hand, manufacturers may well lose out because they have been protected by EU trade barriers and regulations that discriminate against manufacturers elsewhere. Farmers might also suffer since they have received substantial price support from the EU.

Minford's empirical research has estimated that leaving the EU will produce a 4% gain in GDP and living standards. There are further benefits arising from dumping EU legislation and being able to control the mass immigration of unskilled labour into the UK.

Source: Daily Telegraph, 5 August 2016.

1 a Describe the benefits of free trade. **[4]**

  b Explain the ways in which EU membership can lead to trade creation and trade diversion. **[4]**

  c Suppose the EU imposes a 10% tariff on imports of vehicles manufactured in the UK. Use a diagram to analyse the effects on the market for UK vehicles in the EU. **[4]**

  d To what extent do you agree with Minford's view that 'withdrawing from the single market and achieving unilateral free trade, will reap huge gains for the UK economy'. **[8]**

Balance of Payments, Japan

In July 2016, Japan's current account balance was in surplus at ¥1448 bn. This was around 4% of annual GDP. In such a situation, economic theory determines that the yen will appreciate on the foreign exchange market which is bad news yet again for Japanese manufacturers.

Japan's current account has historically been in surplus, mainly due to a trading surplus. More recently, the Income Account has become more important in assuring this surplus as the trading account surplus has fallen, even to a deficit for a short period.

Figure 4.3 below shows two aspects of Japan's balance of payments from 2010 to 2016.

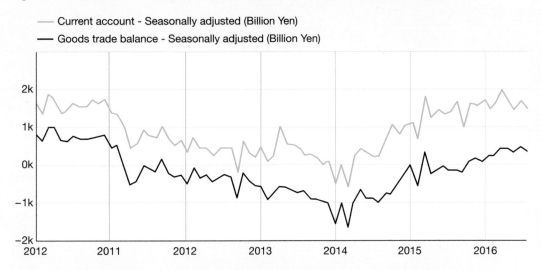

—— Current account - Seasonally adjusted (Billion Yen)
—— Goods trade balance - Seasonally adjusted (Billion Yen)

Figure 4.3 Current account and goods trade balance, 2010–2016

Source: Japan Macro Advisors, September 2016.

2 **a** Describe the relationship between Japan's current account balance and trade balance in goods since 2010. **[3]**

b State and explain **two** items that might be included in the Income Account of Japan's balance of payments. **[4]**

c **i** Explain the likely effects of a rising yen on Japan's balance of payments. **[4]**

ii Explain how a rising yen affects Japan's terms of trade. **[3]**

d Discuss the possible impact of a rising yen on the macroeconomy of Japan. **[6]**

Structured essay questions

1 **a** Using an AD/AS diagram, explain how an excessive increase in government spending along with improved labour productivity might affect the general price level in an economy. **[8]**

b In 2015 the annual rate of inflation in an economy was 10%. Comment on the likely internal and external consequences, saying which you feel to be most serious. **[12]**

2 Assume in a two-country, two-product world that one economy is more efficient at producing both products.

a Explain how the efficient economy can benefit from specialisation and trade with the less efficient economy. **[8]**

b Evaluate the economic reasons that the less efficient economy might offer to justify protection of its industries. **[12]**

Cambridge International AS and A Level Economics 9708 Paper 21 Q4 October/November 2015.

3 **a** Using diagrams, explain why exchange rates can vary in a floating exchange rate system. **[8]**

b Discuss the extent to which a devaluation of the exchange rate can overcome a disequilibrium in an economy's balance of payments. **[12]**

TIP
The stem of the question indicates absolute advantage in both products. Part **(a)** therefore requires an explanation of how comparative advantage applies.

61

4 a Explain the ways in which a developing economy might protect its domestic industries from foreign competition. **[8]**

b Comment on the extent to which these ways might differ for a developed economy. **[12]**

5 a Explain what might cause an improvement in the terms of trade of an economy. **[8]**

b Discuss why the terms of trade of most developing economies have deteriorated over the past few years. **[12]**

6 a Using examples, describe the components on the balance of payments as defined by the IMF/OECD. **[8]**

b Comment upon the consequences for the domestic economy of a persistent deficit in the current account of a country's balance of payments. **[12]**

Multiple choice questions

1 Which of the following is **not** a cause of cost-push inflation?

A A depreciation of the external value of the currency.

B An increase in indirect taxation on consumer goods.

C An increase in government spending on health care.

D An increase in the global price of oil.

2 Figure 4.4 shows a fall in aggregate demand in an economy from AD to AD_1. Which of the following is likely to have caused this?

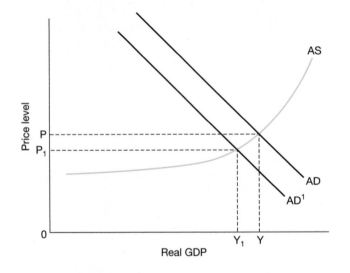

Figure 4.4 Showing a fall in aggregate demand

A A rise in the exchange rate of a country's currency.

B A rise in the minimum threshold for paying income tax.

C A fall in interest rates.

D A fall in net migration.

3   An economy has devalued its currency on the foreign exchange market in order to improve the current account of its balance of payments. Which of the combinations of price elasticities in the table below is most likely to produce the largest improvement?

	P_{ed} exports	P_{ed} imports
A	0.5	0.3
B	1.6	0.3
C	1.0	1.0
D	2.4	1.0

4   The table below shows the annual percentage changes in consumer prices in an economy over a five-year period.

Year	1	2	3	4	5
% change in consumer prices	−1.0	2.4	3.5	5.0	3.4

Table 4.3.

Which of these statements is **not** correct?

A   Consumer prices increased annually from year 2 to year 5.

B   Consumer prices in year 2 were greater than in year 1.

C   Consumer prices in year 5 were less than in year 4.

D   Consumer prices increased most in year 4.

5   An economy has a deficit on the current account of its balance of payments. What may cause this deficit to get worse?

A   A 5% cut in government spending.

B   A 5% depreciation in the economy's exchange rate.

C   A 5% tariff on imports of consumer goods.

D   A 5% increase in the price of essential raw materials.

Think like an economist

Key economic myth

The reason why countries join a customs union such as the EU is that experience has shown that all member states benefit from the internal free trade and common external tariff.

This is not entirely true. Some economies benefit enormously – these are invariably those that are more efficient and have the products and expertise to make the most of the opportunities presented by tariff-free access to a larger market. Other less efficient countries are likely to struggle and there is little they can do about it, certainly in the short term. The recent experience of the Mediterranean economies (Greece, Portugal and Spain) within the EU is indicative.

Key economists

David Ricardo's contribution to economics is widespread, covering micro as well as macroeconomic topics. He is best known for his opposition to protectionism at a time when this was a prevailing force in international trade. In Great Britain, for example, the so-called Corn Laws restricted wheat imports, even at times of shortage. Ricardo strongly argued in favour of free trade through the concept of comparative costs. This is now more widely known as the principle of comparative advantage – his simple 2 × 2 model showed the gains from trade and how countries should specialise in producing those goods for which they have lower comparative costs. This simple principle underpins today's case for universal free trade as promoted by most economists and the World Trade Organization.

Much later than Ricardo, **Jacob Viner** also refuted protectionist policies and is best known for his work on customs unions. He developed the concepts of trade creation and trade diversion as a means of understanding the trade effects of when countries form a customs union such as what was at that time the recently formed European Economic Community. Viner's work made clear that there were costs as well as benefits to trade for members of the customs union, arguing that in some respects it was an example of 'second best' when compared to universal free trade.

Key economic diagram

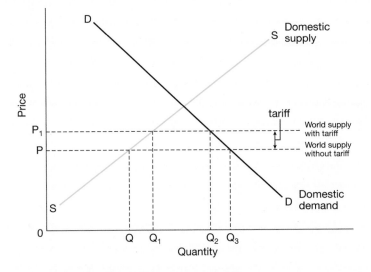

Figure 4.5 The effect of imposing a tariff

Key points:

- A tariff, which is an indirect tax on imports, increases prices for non-domestic suppliers.
- This benefits domestic suppliers and their output or supply increases since they are more price competitive.
- Domestic consumers though lose out; they have to pay a higher price, P_1, whereas before they paid P.
- Moreover, their consumption falls by $Q_3 - Q_2$ whilst domestic production increases from Q to Q_1.
- This represents a loss in consumer surplus as consumers end up buying less at a higher price.
- There is also an increase in producer surplus but this is less than the loss of consumer surplus.

Key economic issue

An important issue for economists is whether or not to protect domestic industries from foreign competition – especially for developing and emerging economies, which rely very heavily on more developed economies for their international trade.

An age-old argument for protection is the infant industry or sunrise industry argument. It is believed that trade restrictions on competitor imports will help such industries to grow, become efficient and able to compete in global markets. So, in the short term especially, protection can be a good thing.

For developed economies, the argument is different. Here, dumping is an issue as evidenced recently by the serious problems facing the UK steel industry in the wake of cheap imported steel from China. A tariff on Chinese steel might on the surface help but it is more likely to do harm to domestic users of UK steel since they will have to pay higher prices for both Chinese imports and domestically produced steel.

Key economic policy

Universal free trade is an ideal enshrined in the role of the World Trade Organization, an international governmental body with 162 members. Its main objective is to abolish import tariffs and other barriers to free trade amongst its members. It therefore has its roots in the arguments against protection put forward by economists well over 200 years ago.

The WTO has in many respects been successful, given the huge increase in the volume and value of international trade, a catalyst for globalisation. Import tariffs on manufactured goods amongst industrialised countries have fallen significantly due to various 'rounds' of talks between members. However, it has been much less successful in freeing up trade in agricultural products, much to the concern of many developing countries who also complain about the subsidies given to agriculture in developed economies like the EU.

A relatively new initiative is that of multilateralism, whereby there is a trade agreement between two or more countries who are members of the WTO. A recent example is the 2016 Trans-Pacific Partnership between 12 Pacific Rim countries led by Australia, Japan and the USA. In line with WTO principles, they reached agreement to cut tariffs and set common standards for trade amongst members. This was before the US withdrew following the election of President Trump.

Review your answer

Read the question below, think about it and then write your own answer. After you have done this, study the advice below and see if you can improve your answer.

Question

a *Explain how exchange rates are determined in different types of exchange rate system.* **[12]**

b *For a country of your choice, assess whether 'depreciation is good, appreciation is bad' for the domestic and external economy.* **[13]**

Advice on how to answer this question

Part **(a)** is straightforward and your answer should include:

- a simple definition of an exchange rate. Avoid any confusion with interest rate
- an explanation of how a floating exchange rate works, ideally with a diagram
- an explanation of how a fixed exchange rate system works
- mention of a managed floating exchange rate.

Part **(b)** has two tasks. These are:

i to say whether depreciation is good and appreciation is bad for both the domestic and external economy

ii to make some reference to a country of your choice, ideally your own if you know what has happened recently to the exchange rate. Do not ignore this aspect of the question.

Your answer can be structured as follows:

- an analysis of how depreciation affects the domestic and external economy

- an analysis of how appreciation affects the domestic and external economy

- consideration of how the exchange rate of a country of your choice has either depreciated or appreciated its exchange rate and what effects this has had

- your final paragraph should make clear whether you agree with the statement in general terms and with respect to your own country; a very good answer will say to what extent the experience of your country is typical.

(AS Level)

Learning outcomes

The exercises in this chapter will help you to practise what you have learnt about:

- the aims of macroeconomic policy
- what is meant by fiscal, monetary and supply-side policies
- the aims and instruments of each policy
- how fiscal, monetary and supply-side policies may correct a balance of payments disequilibrium
- the factors that influence the effectiveness of fiscal, monetary and supply-side policies to correct a balance of payments disequilibrium
- how fiscal, monetary and supply-side policies may correct inflation and deflation
- the factors that influence the effectiveness of fiscal, monetary and supply-side policies to correct inflation and deflation.

REMEMBER
The content of this chapter builds upon that contained in Chapter 4. Do note the higher order, analysis and evaluation, assessment objectives.

KEY TERMS

You should **know and understand** what is meant by the following key terms. These terms are defined in Chapter 5 of the course book.

Fiscal policy	**Monetary policy**
Discretionary fiscal policy	**Interest rate**
Automatic stabilisers	**Money supply**
Budget	**Supply-side policy**
Cyclical budget deficit	**Expenditure switching policy**
Structural budget deficit	**Expenditure dampening or reducing policy**

TIP
Make sure you really understand aggregate demand and aggregate supply. These concepts are central to the content of this chapter.

Exercises

1   Complete the table below for the ways in which governments can intervene in the macroeconomy in order to meet the three objectives that are shown.

Objective / Type of policy	Balance of payments equilibrium	Low and stable inflation	To combat deflation
Fiscal			
Monetary			
Supply-side			
Direct controls			

68

2 Consider Figures 5.1a and b.

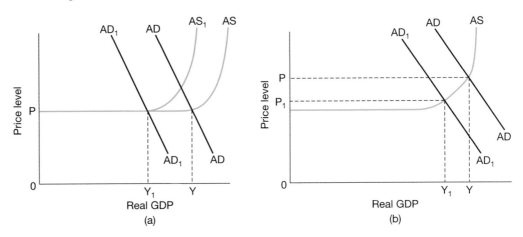

Figure 5.1 AD/AS diagrams

For each diagram, make a few notes on:

i what each diagram shows

ii what might have brought about the changes shown

iii why the changes may not always be effective.

3 Egypt: Balance of Payments (US$m)

	2014/15[+]	2015/16[+]
Exports	17,097	13,406
– petroleum	6,938	4,211
– other	10,159	9,195
Imports	−46,643	−42,727
– petroleum	−9,239	−7,072
– other	−37,404	−35,655
Services receipts (net)	4,252	2,408
– travel (net)	2,997	344
Current Account Balance	−8,345	−14,470
Financial and Capital Account	6,649	13,907
Net errors and omissions	650	−3,078
Overall Balance	−1,046	−3,641

+ - period July-March

Table 5.1 Egypt's balance of power

a What evidence is there that the balance of payments of Egypt is in disequilibrium? **[Ap]**

b Suggest policies that the Egyptian government might use to correct the disequilibrium. **[A]**

4 In September 2016, the UK government announced that it was keen for more teenagers to become apprentices in industries such as construction, engineering, transport, hotels and catering.

   a Analyse how an increase in the number of apprentices in the UK is likely to affect real GDP. **[A]**

   b Consider the possible ways in which the number of new apprentices might be increased. **[E]**

5 Malaysia has started to remove import taxes on vehicles produced in Australia and Japan under a recent agreement signed with its ASEAN partners.

   a Analyse the likely effects of removing these import taxes on Malaysia's macroeconomy. **[A]**

   b Comment upon whether the removal of import taxes is likely to have a negative impact on Malaysian vehicle manufacturers. **[E]**

6 In March 2016, the *Economic Times* reported that 'India's inflation has eased and the central bank is expected to cut interest rates'.

   a Explain how a fall in interest rates is likely to affect the rate of inflation in India. **[A]**

   b Discuss whether monetary policy is the best way to control inflation. **[E]**

Exam-style questions

Data response

Disequilibrium in Pakistan's balance of trade

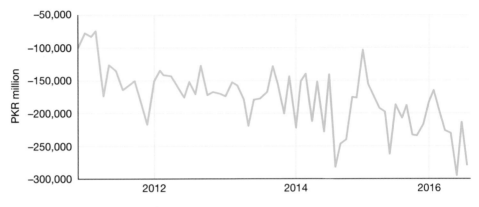

Figure 5.2 Pakistan's balance of trade

Pakistan's balance of trade position is in serious disequilibrium despite falling oil prices (see Figure 5.2). In the last half of 2015, exports plunged to $10.3bn, 14.4% less than in the same period last year. Imports also fell, mainly due to the drop in world oil prices. At $22.2bn they were 7.9% down. The one positive for Pakistan's economy was that Pakistani workers overseas remitted almost $10bn back home in the same period.

A particular problem has been the value of the exchange rate of the rupee against the US dollar. The International Monetary fund believe that the rupee is overvalued by 5–20%.
This discrepancy clearly undermines Pakistan's competitiveness and stifles its ability to make economic reforms.

A new cause for concern is the Trans Pacific Partnership (TPP). Led by the USA, Australia and New Zealand, 12 countries have signed up to cut tariffs and set common standards for trade amongst members. Vietnam, one of Pakistan's main trade competitors, is a member of the TPP. This could well prove damaging to Pakistan's already fragile economy.

Source: *Express Tribune*, 13 January 2016 (adapted).

a **i** Describe and account for the trend in Pakistan's balance of trade from 2011 to 2016. **[4]**

    ii Explain how remittances from Pakistani workers overseas contribute to the balance of payments of Pakistan. **[2]**

b Analyse the effects of a strong rupee on Pakistan's balance of trade. **[4]**

c Explain why non-membership of the TPP might be damaging for Pakistan's economy. **[4]**

d Discuss the policies that Pakistan might use to correct its balance of trade disequilibrium. **[6]**

Essay questions

1 **a** Outline the components of aggregate demand and explain **one** cause of an increase and **one** cause of a decrease in aggregate demand in an economy. **[8]**

    b Compare two policies that may be considered to solve the problem of demand-pull inflation and evaluate which is likely to be the more effective. **[12]**

TIP
Note that Q1 draws upon the content of Chapter 4 as well as Chapter 5. This type of question can be expected. Q2 though draws wholly on the content of Chapter 5.

2 a Using examples, explain the instruments of fiscal policy. **[8]**

   b Discuss the advantages and disadvantages of fiscal policy and comment on its effectiveness in an economy that is facing disequilibrium in its balance of payments. **[12]**

3 a Using examples, distinguish between short-run and long-run supply-side policies. **[8]**

   b An economy is experiencing on-going balance of trade deficits, mainly because its exports are not price competitive. Suggest how supply-side policies might help to restore competitiveness. Consider their likely effectiveness. **[12]**

Multiple choice questions

1 Which of these is **not** a fiscal policy instrument?

   A A fall in the rate of income tax.

   B An increase in government spending on education.

   C A rise in the central bank's interest rate.

   D The introduction of a new general service tax on restaurant meals.

2 An automatic stabiliser is:

   A A type of tax that reduces with fluctuations in real GDP.

   B A policy measure that automatically occurs once unemployment increases above a certain annual rate.

   C A type of tax or government expenditure that changes automatically with fluctuations in real GDP.

   D A type of tax that remains the same irrespective of changes in real GDP.

3 An economy has a deficit on the current account of its balance of payments. Which of the following is least likely to lead to an improvement in this deficit?

   A A planned devaluation of the currency.

   B A new 10% tariff on imports that have a wide range of domestic substitutes.

   C An increase in government spending.

   D An increase in price of essential oil imports.

4 Which one of these can be classified as a supply-side measure designed to expand aggregate supply?

   A An increase in government spending for new apprenticeships.

   B A reduction in the rate of general sales tax.

   C An increase in investment from foreign-owned companies.

   D A reduction in the rate of interest.

5 Which of these is an example of an expenditure-reducing policy to correct a balance of trade deficit?

   A A 5% tariff on imported clothing.

   B An increase in the basic rate of income tax.

   C An increased quota on imported clothing.

   D A subsidy paid to local clothing producers.

Think like an economist

Key economic myth

Fiscal and monetary policies by controlling aggregate demand provide governments with all they need to achieve their macroeconomic aims.

This might have been the case a generation ago but it is most certainly not true today. As all economies become more complex and globally dependent, a range of policies is required in order to manage the macroeconomy in an appropriate way. Supply-side policies are particularly important in raising output, a fundamental objective in all types of economy.

Key diagrams

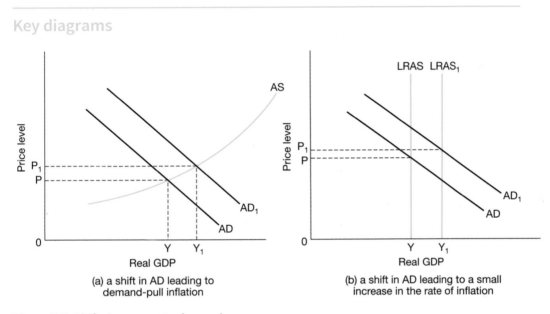

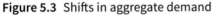

(a) a shift in AD leading to demand-pull inflation

(b) a shift in AD leading to a small increase in the rate of inflation

Figure 5.3 Shifts in aggregate demand

Figure 5.3a shows the usual explanation of demand-pull inflation – an increase in aggregate demand from AD to AD₁ leads to an increase in the price level from P to P₁. This is a short-run situation which can usually be reversed through a tight fiscal or monetary policy.

Figure 5.3b shows a mild increase in inflation. The increase in aggregate demand from AD to AD₁ has largely been offset by an increase in long-run aggregate supply from LRAS to LRAS₁.

Key economic issue

A key economic issue facing individuals as well as economies is how much should be spent on education and training. From a government's standpoint, there is the opportunity cost of this expenditure relative to other demands on its resources. A key factor is the increase in future economic potential arising from certain types of educational expenditure and their impact in shifting aggregate supply. This also applies to an individual especially in countries where education has to be paid for.

73

Key economist

Jan Tinbergen was a Dutch economist who developed the idea of modelling the macroeconomy as a means of assisting policy makers. He believed that there should be targets for the main macroeconomic variables and that these should be influenced by politicians and others with responsibility for economic policy. The models required an input of the various fiscal and monetary policies available in order to forecast their impact with respect to these targets. This concept underpins the monetary policy of many central banks; an inflation target of say 2% is applied as the main target for managing the macroeconomy.

Key economic policy

The long-term well-being of any economy depends on its success in applying supply-side policies to increase aggregate supply and hence output. These policies work through particular product and factor markets to improve economic performance and competitiveness.

There is no single supply-side policy instrument. There are many, covering:

- labour markets: restrictions on power of trade unions, minimum wages, migration

- education and training: raising school leaving age, investment in technical training, retraining redundant workers

- improving infrastructure: new motorways, high speed rail, reliable water and power supplies

- promoting competition through privatisation and deregulation

- incentives to encourage more people to work: income tax changes, welfare benefits

- incentives to increase exports.

The ways in which supply-side policies work is different to those applying to fiscal and monetary policies, which basically operate via changes in aggregate demand.

Review your answers

1   **a**   Explain the instruments of monetary policy. **[8]**

    b   Monetarists maintain that an increase in the money supply is the only true cause of inflation … it therefore follows that monetary policy alone can control inflation.

       Discuss this view. **[12]**

Advice on how to answer this question

This question draws largely upon the content of Chapter 5; however, part **(b)** requires some knowledge of the causes of inflation contained in Chapter 4.

Part **(a)** is straightforward and uses the words in the syllabus. You need to explain each of the three instruments of monetary policy namely:

- the interest rate

- the money supply

- the exchange rate (if applicable).

After a simple description, a good approach is to explain how changes in each affect aggregate demand. This can then provide a link to your answer to part **(b)**.

Part **(b)** is more difficult since it is asking you to discuss the view that the instruments you explained in part **(a)** are the only ways in which inflation can be controlled. Supporters of fiscal policies will clearly argue that this is not the case. Your answer to this part could be structured as follows:

- An analysis of how an increase in interest rates, a reduction in the money supply and an appreciation of the exchange rate lead to a reduction in aggregate demand and hence a fall in the rate of inflation. An AD/AS diagram can be used.

- One or two sentences could be written on cost-push causes of inflation; an analysis OF how a reduction in government spending and/or an increase in certain types of taxation can reduce aggregate demand and hence control inflation could be provided.

- The discussion could argue that it really depends on the perceived causes of inflation and how these vary from one economy to another and over time.

- Make sure your conclusion is clear and balanced. A very good conclusion should argue which of the two approaches is most valid at the present time.

allocation (A Level)

Learning outcomes

The exercises in this chapter will help you to practise what you have learnt about:

- what economists mean by an efficient resource allocation and why this is an important microeconomic concept
- what is meant by economic efficiency
- what is meant by productive and allocative efficiency, Pareto optimality and dynamic efficiency
- the reasons for market failure
- what is meant by positive and negative externalities and why they lead to an inefficient allocation of resources
- private costs, external costs and social costs; private benefits, external benefits and social benefits
- how cost-benefit analysis can be used as an aid to decision-making.

KEY TERMS

You should **know and understand** what is meant by the following key terms. These terms are defined in Chapter 6 of the course book.

Economic efficiency	Private costs
Productive efficiency	External costs
Allocative efficiency	Social benefits
Pareto optimality	Private benefits
Externality	External benefits
Negative externality	Cost-benefit analysis
Positive externality	Shadow price
Social costs	

Exercises

1   Insert a few words to complete the phrases below.

In simple terms, efficiency can be described as …… Economic efficiency is more specific and is defined as …… Productive efficiency occurs when ……; allocative efficiency is different and it is where …… Perfect competition ensures an efficient allocation of resources because …… This is not true for monopoly since ……

2   Figure 6.1 shows four short-run average cost curves, each of which represents a different scale of operation of a firm.

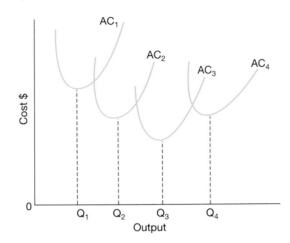

Figure 6.1 Four short-run average cost curves

a   What is the most efficient level of output for the firm to produce? Why?

b   If the firm were to expand its scale of operations beyond this point, what would result?

3   Market failure exists when a market, left to its own devices and with no government intervention, fails to make the optimum use of scarce resources.

Say which of the following are indicative of market failure and write a few words to justify your choice.

a   Discarding used batteries in the gutter.

b   A garage that does not have sufficient cars to meet demand.

c   An infant immunisation programme to combat a serious illness.

d   A chemical manufacturer that is free to pollute the environment around its factory.

e   Extensive road traffic congestion in a city that lacks an efficient mass transit system.

4   A positive externality is where the production or consumption of goods and services results in an external benefit to a third party who has not taken part in the activity.

a   In the space below, give some examples of positive externalities from your own country.

1.

2.

3.

4.

5.

6.

77

b In each case, justify your example in a few words.

c Draw diagrams to show why, when there are positive externalities, there is under-consumption and under-provision in the market.

5 A negative externality occurs when the production or consumption of goods and services results in an external cost to a third party who has not taken part in the activity.

a In the space below, give some examples of negative externalities from your own country.

1.

2.

3.

4.

5.

6.

b In each case, justify your example in a few words.

c Draw diagrams to show why, when there are negative externalities, there is overconsumption and overprovision in the market.

6 A fish processing factory discharges fumes that affect the quality of life of people living close by. The firm aims to maximise its profits. The data in Table 6.1 describe this situation after a pollution tax equal to marginal external cost has been levied on the factory.

Output (tonnes)	Marginal private cost ($'000)	Marginal revenue ($'000)	Marginal external cost ($'000)
10	30	66	18
20	30	60	21
30	30	54	24
40	30	48	27
50	30	42	30
60	30	36	33
70	30	30	36
80	30	24	39

Table 6.1

What is the change in output after the tax has been imposed? Give a brief explanation.

7 For many years, UNICEF has spent large sums of money providing clean water facilities and educating people in poor developing economies on how to best use this vital resource.

a Explain the private, external and social benefits involved in providing clean water to people in poor developing economies. **[A]**

b Comment upon how UNICEF might apply cost-benefit analysis to prioritise where clean water facilities should be provided. **[E]**

Exam-style questions

Data response question

The Hong Kong-Zuhai-Macao Bridge

The Hong Kong-Zhuhai-Macao Bridge, currently under construction, is the largest infrastructure project in Asia to date. When completed, it will be the longest cross-sea road bridge in the world, connecting Hong Kong's Lantau Island with Guangdong Zuhai on the Chinese mainland and Macao, the former Portuguese island.

The project is a huge, complex engineering challenge. It is hardly surprising therefore that its construction costs of HK$117bn have increased and the original opening date of 2016 seems more likely to be 2020. When operational, the bridge will reduce travel times to Lantau Island, location of Hong Kong's international airport; Macao, which is currently only accessible by ferry, will be physically integrated into the Pearl River delta region and the travel time from Hong Kong will be around 30 minutes compared to more than 3 hours at present.

The original cost-benefit assessment followed a standard methodology and was based on the projected direct economic benefits to road passengers and to freight users in relation to the total costs. This resulted in an estimated rate of return of 8.8%, which compared favourably with other rail and road schemes under construction in Hong Kong.

The cost-benefit study stressed the strategic and indirect benefits of the bridge to local economies, although no attempt was made to quantify them.

The construction of the bridge is controversial. Some economists have argued that the money could be better used for other infrastructure projects, not least because the benefits are by no means certain.

a Describe some of the 'direct' economic benefits to road passengers and freight users and explain how these might be calculated. **[6]**

b i Describe what is meant by a rate of return. **[2]**

ii Explain how the stated rate of return might change given that its construction costs have increased to more than HK$117bn. **[2]**

c Explain some of the possible indirect benefits of the bridge. **[4]**

d Comment on whether you feel that the bridge is justified. **[6]**

Essay questions

1 There was a period when many publicly owned enterprises were privatised. Investors said that privatisation would increase competition, encourage greater efficiency and raise profits.

a Explain what is meant by economic efficiency. **[12]**

b Discuss how the privatisation of an industry might affect economic efficiency. **[13]**

Cambridge International AS and A Level Economics 9708, Paper 41 Q2 October/November 2015.

> **REMEMBER**
> You should note that part **(b)** of this question requires some knowledge of privatisation from AS Level as well as the content of Government microeconomic intervention.

2   Explain what is meant by an efficient allocation of resources and discuss why the market mechanism invariably fails to produce the best allocation of resources. **[25]**

3   **a**   Explain main stages in a cost-benefit analysis, drawing upon an example of your choice. **[12]**

    b   Discuss why despite a favourable cost-benefit analysis, the decision may be taken to **not** proceed with a particular project. **[13]**

Multiple choice questions

1   The table below shows the number of units of labour and capital that are required to produce a given quantity of output. A unit of labour costs $100 and a unit of capital costs $400.

Which of the combinations is productively efficient?

	Output	Labour	Capital
A	10	4	1
B	20	7	2
C	30	10	3
D	40	15	4

2   Which one of these situations is **not** a reason for market failure?

    A   The banning of smoking in local food courts.

    B   The lack of information on what is in a take-away food item.

    C   The convenience store does not find it profitable to stock packet rice.

    D   The provision of free education for children under 16 years of age.

3   A firm is dynamically efficient when:

    A   Its long-run average cost curve shifts downwards.

    B   It produces a new range of exciting products.

    C   It makes large profits for its shareholders.

    D   It can respond quickly to change in the market.

4   A huge pile of rubber tyres is set on fire by owners who want to dispose of them. Which of the following is **not** a negative externality associated with this action?

    A   Residents in a nearby apartment block have left their windows open and have to clean up.

    B   The owner's office building is destroyed.

    C   The dense smoke causes a road accident in which a pedestrian is injured.

    D   A local football match has to be cancelled.

5 The table below shows the respective total benefits, total costs and capital cost of four new stretches of a road. Which option provides the most efficient use of resources?

	Total benefits ($m)	Total costs ($m)	Capital cost ($m)
A	50	40	2
B	100	60	10
C	20	5	2
D	30	20	5

Improve your answer

Read the question and answer below and see how you can improve it using the suggestions that follow.

Question

Using examples, explain what is meant by a positive externality and consider how the production and consumption of goods and services that produce positive externalities might be increased. **[25]**

Let me first of all say what a positive externality is. This is a term that is used in economics to describe a situation where someone is able to benefit from what somebody else has provided and where they have not had to pay for it. There is what is known as an external benefit or positive externality.

A few examples will help you to see what I mean. An inoculation against a disease such as malaria or polio benefits the individual who receives it. It also means that other people who you meet will not have as great a risk of getting the disease. Getting a good education is another example. Stopping at school and taking A Levels should help me get a good job, which will then help my economy to also benefit. If I had left school earlier, I may have ended up with a job with poor pay or not even managed to get a job at all. In both of these cases, the social benefit to the economy exceeds the private benefit.

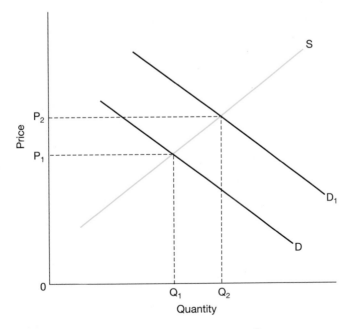

Figure 6.2 Diagram to show positive externality

81

The examples I have given are called merit goods. This is because everybody benefits from them – everyone is healthier and better educated. The problem, however, is that not everybody can afford to pay school fees or visit the doctor to get an inoculation. Because of this, governments like my own decide to provide a minimum level of education. The money for this comes from the taxes we pay on high incomes and the general sales tax. The government also pays for babies to be inoculated.

Another way that governments have to increase the consumption of these merit goods is for them to be subsidised. This means that consumers end up paying a lower price. The subsidy is paid to the private owners of a school. This means poorer kids may be able to now go to school. The really poor children may end up not paying anything at all. Their fees will be paid by the government to the school. This must be a good thing to happen.

There is also the problem of opportunity cost. The government has to be careful in these situations since it has only a fixed amount to spend on activities like health and education. When spending, it could help if it had done a cost-benefit study of the problems.

Suggestions on how to improve this answer

> **REMEMBER**
> What was said about how to write in an analytical way and how to structure effective answers to essay questions.

- The answer is written in a 'chatty' style. This should be avoided especially at A Level. It is also not good style to use 'me' and 'I' in your answer.

- The style of writing gets better after the diagram but the diagram, which is simple for A Level, is not referred to in the answer. Also, the diagram shows positive consumption externalities; there ought to be a second diagram showing positive production externalities.

> **REMEMBER**
> Diagrams are an essential part of the economist's tool kit. They only add value to an essay answer when they are explicitly referred to.

- The examples are appropriate but could be expanded a little.

- The distinction between production and consumption positive externalities needs to be made clearer.

- The last paragraph could benefit from more in-depth analysis.

- There is no concluding paragraph.

Learning outcomes

The exercises in this chapter will help you to practise what you have learnt about:

- the law of diminishing marginal utility and how to understand its relationship to the derivation of an individual demand schedule
- the limitations of marginal utility theory and why consumers are not always rational
- how indifference curves can be used to represent what consumers want
- what a budget line is and how it can be used to show the income and substitution effects of a price change
- the short-run production function: fixed and variable factors of production; total product, average product and marginal product
- the law of diminishing returns; average cost, marginal cost
- how to apply the long-run production function and returns to scale
- the shape of the long-run average cost curve
- how to apply the economies of scale, internal and external; diseconomies of scale
- how to define total, average and marginal revenue
- the difference between normal and abnormal profit
- what is meant by market structure and how it can be explained and applied
- the difference between perfect and imperfect competition
- how to analyse and evaluate the market structures of monopoly, monopolistic competition, oligopoly and natural monopoly
- what is meant by contestable markets and how to evaluate the implications of contestability in a market
- reasons for the growth and survival of small firms
- what is meant by profit maximisation and why there are other objectives of firms
- how firms make pricing decisions
- how it is possible to compare the performance of firms.

83

KEY TERMS

You should **know and understand** what is meant by the following key terms. These terms are defined in Chapter 7 of the course book.

Utility	Diminishing returns	Small and medium enterprises	Price leadership
Total utility	Firm	Industry	Cartel
Marginal utility	Profit maximisation	Multinational corporations	X-inefficiency
Diminishing marginal utility	Fixed costs	Market structure	Contestable market
Equimarginal principle	Variable costs	Barriers to entry	Economies of scope
Budget line	Increasing returns to scale	Perfect competition	Diversification
Substitution effect	Diminishing returns to scale	Monopoly	Horizontal integration
Income effect	Economies of scale	Monopolistic competition	Vertical integration
Indifference curve	Diseconomies of scale	Oligopoly	Sales revenue maximisation
Marginal rate of substitution	External economies of scale	Imperfect competition	Sales maximisation
Isoquant	Minimum efficient scale	Natural monopoly	Satisficing
Total product	Profit	Barrier to exit	Game theory
Production function	Normal profit	Limit pricing	Kinked demand curve
Marginal product	Abnormal profit	Horizontal integration	

REMEMBER
This is an
important part of
the microeconomic
A Level syllabus.
You should be
aware of this when
planning your
revision.

Exercises

1 Each of the statements below refer to indifference curves, budget lines and consumer choice.
For each, say whether it is 'true' or 'false'.

   i   Marginal utility theory is based on the assumption that consumers always act in a
rational way.

   ii An indifference curve always slopes downwards and to the right because consumers always
prefer to buy more rather than less.

   iii An individual consumer maximises utility where the budget line meets an indifference curve.

   iv Indifference curves never intersect if consumers are rational and consistent in their choices.

   v   The slope of the budget line depends on the real income of the consumer.

   vi The substitution effect of an increase in price of a good always reduces the quantity
demanded of that good.

   vii Following an increase in price of a good, the income effect is greater than the substitution
effect. This means that the good is a normal good.

2

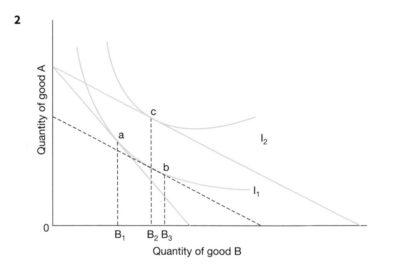

Figure 7.1 Indifference curve diagram

The indifference curve diagram in Figure 7.1 shows what happens when the price of an inferior
good, B, falls. From the diagram, identify the substitution and income effects of the price change
and say what each means.

3 The data below show a typical cost structure for producing a take-away pizza in a city centre
franchised retailer. The retail price of the pizza is $5.

	Costs $ (per pizza)
Rent	1.20
Labour	0.50
Heating, lighting	0.40
Community charges	1.10
Food ingredients	0.50
Packaging	0.30
Profit	1.00

Table 7.1 Typical cost structure for producing a take-away pizza

i   Calculate the average fixed costs and average variable costs of producing a pizza.

ii Suppose the rent increases to $2.50 per pizza. Explain how this might affect the firm's decision whether to remain at this location in the short run and in the long run.

4 Economies of scale are the benefits gained from falling long-run average costs as output increases.

i   Take the case of a supermarket company that continues to increase its scale of operations. In the table below, suggest some examples of economies of scale that may apply.

Type	Examples
Purchasing economies	
Marketing economies	
Managerial economies	
Technological economies	
Financial economies	
Risk-bearing economies	

ii Under what circumstances might there be diseconomies of scale?

5 A firm is operating in a perfectly competitive industry. Its cost curves are shown in Figure 7.2. The market price is P.

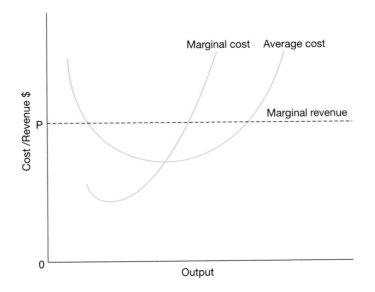

Figure 7.2 Competitive industry cost curves

i On the diagram:

  – show the level of output where profits are maximised

  – show the profits made by the firm at this level of output.

ii Does this represent the short-run or long-run equilibrium position? Explain your answer.

iii If the market demand falls, how would this affect the firm?

6 For each of the examples below, say which is the most likely market structure.

  i A few petroleum refining companies supplying a national market.

  ii A railway company which operates the only service between two cities.

  iii Hawkers' food stalls selling local food at similar prices.

  iv A large number of small farmers each producing rice at identical prices.

  v A company that has a patented product that cannot be legally copied by others.

7 The two pie charts below show what might occur in the UK mobile phone network industry if the Hong Kong based company Hutchison – which operates Three – is allowed to acquire O_2.

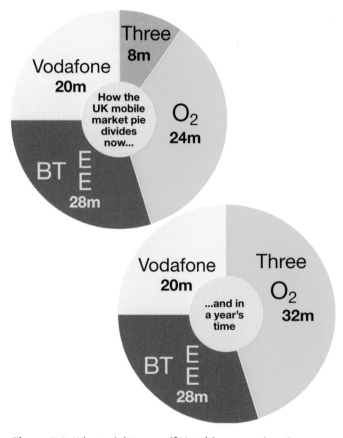

Figure 7.3 What might occur if Hutchison acquires O_2

Assume that Three takes over O_2. As well as market share, what other evidence would you need to show that this industry is an oligopoly?

8 Contestability is a set of conditions that can apply in any market structure.

Take a market in your own country and see if it matches any of the important features of a contestable market. Use the table below.

Features	Evidence
Free cost entry/ barriers to entry	
Normal profits	
Potential entrants	
Number and size of firms	
Regulations in place	

TIP

As well as considering at least two theories, remember to refer to specific examples of oligopolistic behaviour.

9 a Use a kinked demand curve diagram to analyse how an oligopolistic firm behaves in a market where there is no collusion. **[A]**

   b Discuss the view that 'it is difficult to put forward one completely acceptable theory of oligopolistic behaviour'. **[E]**

10 a Using examples from your own country, explain some reasons why small firms exist. **[A]**

    b Comment upon the opinion that 'profit maximisation is most unlikely to be the over-riding objective of small firms'. **[E]**

Exam-style questions

Data response question

Multinationals and the global trade in bananas

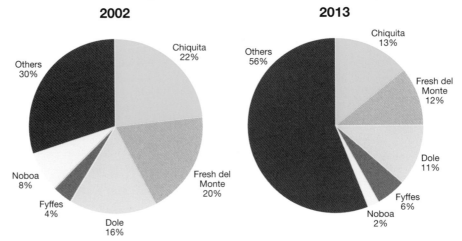

Figure 7.4 Market shares of selected companies in global banana exports by volume

The global trade in bananas is huge. In 2013, it was estimated that banana exports were over 16.5 million tonnes and projected to continue to rise. Around 80% of these exports are from Latin America and the Caribbean, the rest coming increasingly from Africa and Asia. Bananas were particularly popular with consumers in the UK and USA. They are a cheap fruit, easy to eat and contain important vitamins and minerals. Yet behind this facade, there is a history of a bitter trade war and dubious business practices between the main export distributors.

The trade is dominated by the so-called 'Big Four' distributors: Chiquita, Fresh del Monte, Dole and Fyffes. Chiquita and Dole are US-owned, Fresh del Monte is owned by a Jordanian/Palestinian company, whilst Fyffes are based in Ireland. All own or contract plantations in Central and Latin America, have their own sea transport and ripening facilities, and usually their own distribution networks. This control over the supply chain has allowed these companies to benefit from economies of scale. As a consequence, they can sell bananas very cheaply in the USA ('dollar bananas') and in northern Europe. The pie charts above show the change in their market shares between 2002 and 2013.

The business practices of the Big Four have been heavily criticised as being not always in the best interests of consumers and growers. The competitive nature of the export market requires the distribution of cheap, unblemished bananas requiring huge amounts of chemicals in the production, ripening and distribution stages. There has also been regular on-going criticism from an ethical standpoint – only around 12% of the final retail price stays in producing countries, half of which is paid to growers. These concerns have led to an increase in national grower's companies such as Noboa in Columbia and pressure from consumers for more 'fair trade' practices.

Source: Banana Link, December 2015.

a From the information provided, say whether the Big Four distributors have applied vertical or horizontal integration in their businesses. Justify your answer. **[3]**

b i Calculate the four firm concentration ratios for 2002 and 2013. **[2]**

  ii Comment on any differences you have found. **[4]**

c Using a diagram, explain how the Big Four benefit from economies of scale. **[5]**

d Discuss whether the Big Four's behaviour is typical of that of an oligopoly. **[6]**

Essay questions

1 The traditional theory of the firm assumes a single objective for the firm, namely the maximisation of profit.

    a Explain whether a firm with this objective necessarily always makes a profit. **[12]**

    b Discuss how the objective in the traditional theory may be varied in different market structures. **[13]**

Cambridge International AS and A Level Economics 9708, Paper 42, Q5 May/June 2016.

2 a Analyse the relationship between the cost curves of an individual firm and the supply curve of the industry. **[12]**

    b In the long-run, average cost falls with increases in output and, therefore, larger firms are always to be preferred to smaller firms. Do you agree with this opinion? **[13]**

Cambridge International AS and A Level Economics 9708 Paper 41 Q3 October/November 2015.

3 The conventional view that economists have is that monopolies do not work in the best interests of consumers and the economy.

Discuss whether there is any substance in this view. **[25]**

4 a Using an indifference curve diagram, explain how this can be used to analyse how a consumer's demand curve can be derived. **[12]**

    b Discuss why consumers may not always act in a rational way as implied by indifference analysis. **[13]**

5 In 2016, Saudi Arabia wanted members of the OPEC cartel to increase the supply of oil on the global market. Other OPEC members refused to do this.

    a Explain how and why a cartel such as OPEC operates. **[12]**

    b Discuss why Saudi Arabia's policy to increase the supply of oil might not have been acceptable to other members of the cartel. **[13]**

Multiple choice questions

1 A firm that manufactures mechanical diggers has fixed costs of $30,000 per week. The variable cost of each digger is $5,000. Which of the following is correct for the calculation of marginal cost and average cost when the firm manufactures five diggers per week?

	Marginal Cost ($)	Average Cost ($)
A	1,000	11,000
B	5,000	11,,000
C	4,000	12,500
D	5,000	12,500

TIP

The focus of this question is about the behaviour of oligopolists. Note that the pie graphs only show market share not the total size of the export market.

TIP

Indifference curve diagrams are not the easiest to draw. If you are not confident about drawing the diagram correctly, do not attempt the question.

2 Figure 7.5 shows the short-run equilibrium position of a firm in a monopolistically competitive market. Which of the statements below best explains the difference between this short-run equilibrium and the long-run equilibrium position?

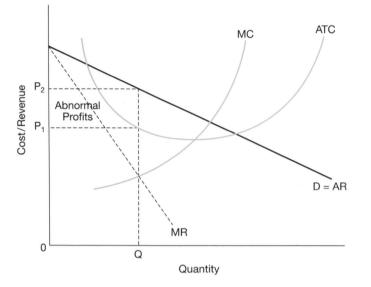

Figure 7.5 The short-run equilibrium position of a firm in a monopolistically competitive market

A Abnormal profits are competed away as new firms enter the market.

B There is no difference between the two positions.

C It is not possible to tell since the long-run price is not given.

D The firm becomes efficient in the long run.

3 The global vehicle manufacturing industry is a typical example of an oligopoly. Which of the characteristics below is least likely to apply as a description of such an oligopoly?

A The amalgamation of firms is unlikely to occur in the future.

B All manufacturers now produce a similar range of vehicles.

C There are substantial barriers to entry for new manufacturers.

D The market is dominated by a small number of firms such as Toyota, VW and Ford.

4 A multinational brewing company has grown its business through acquiring a budget hotel company, a chain of specialist coffee shops and fast food restaurants. How is this process known?

A Vertical integration.   **B** Diversification.

C Economies of scale.   **D** Horizontal integration.

5 A firm has two variable factors of production, labour (L) and raw materials (R). It employs them at fixed prices, P_L and P_R.

AP_L and AP_R and MP_L and MP_R are the average and marginal products of labour and raw materials.

Which of the following represents the way in which the firm should use these factors to minimise the cost of producing a given output?

A $\dfrac{MP_L}{MP_R} = \dfrac{P_L}{P_R}$ **B** $\dfrac{MP_L}{MP_R} = \dfrac{AP_L}{AP_R}$ **C** $\dfrac{AP_L}{P_L} = \dfrac{AP_R}{P_R}$ **D** $\dfrac{MP_L}{P_L} = \dfrac{AP_R}{P_R}$

Think like an economist

Key economic myth

Monopolists always earn abnormal profits

This might be the commonly-held view after studying the market structure of monopoly. However, it is an economic myth – if it is possible for new firms to enter the monopolist's market, then abnormal profits can become normal profits. This outcome is consistent with the idea of a contestable market.

Key economist

The US economist **William J. Baumol** created a form of rebellion in microeconomics when, along with Panzar and Willig, he developed the idea of a contestable market. Their ground-breaking work, subtitled 'an uprising in the theory of industrial structure', stressed that where there was zero cost freedom of entry and exit for new firms in a market, irrespective of its structure, firms would earn no more than normal profits.

The implications of Baumol's work have been far reaching. In particular, it questioned the need for anti-trust regulations in many markets, arguing that deregulation would provide a better, more efficient allocation of resources for consumers and the macroeconomy. Commencing with the US domestic airline market, deregulation has been extensively used to open up a wide range of transport, fuel and power and financial markets to competitive market forces in developed and increasingly, in developing economies.

Key economic diagram

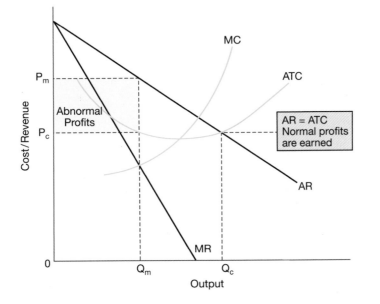

Figure 7.6 Abnormal profits

Key points:

- The diagram indicates that a monopolist earns abnormal profits where MC = MR; price is P_m and output is Q_m.

- The entry of a new competitor into the market would wipe out some if not all of the abnormal profits.

- A monopolist, fearing such entry, would reduce price to P_c; output would increase to Q_c, with only normal profits being earned.

- The result would be the same as if the market were perfectly competitive.

Key economic issue

The conventional views of monopolies, and of many oligopolies, is that they are powerful firms that have excessive control over the markets in which they operate. As price makers, they control the prices paid by consumers and provided they can control costs, they invariably make excessive profits.

More specifically, these issues include:

- Price is higher and output produced is lower in monopoly when compared to a perfectly competitive industry.

- A monopolist is inefficient in terms of allocative and productive efficiency – this is because price is greater than marginal cost and the monopolist produces at a point that is higher than the minimum point on the average total cost curve.

- A lack of competition leads to x-inefficiency whereby the monopolist's costs are actually higher than they would be in a more competitive market.

- Monopolies can be complacent because of their market power and lack incentives to fully engage in research and development.

Although monopolies can provide certain benefits, most economists agree that these are outweighed by the considerable disadvantages as outlined above.

Key economic policy

The criticisms of monopolies and oligopolies and the emergence of support for more contestable markets has attracted the attention of governments and the work of their regulatory bodies such as the Markets Commission in the UK.

Deregulation, especially in cases accompanied by privatisation, has been a key economic policy in promoting contestability in many different types of market, particularly in the services sector. Deregulation has various advantages – with increased competition, consumers can benefit from lower prices and a wider choice, and businesses are able to be more efficient as they are not as restricted by having to comply with endless regulations and overall, economic welfare increases.

In many ways, the UK government has led the way by deregulating and privatising important sectors of the economy such as transport and communications, power and water supplies. Former state-owned manufacturing companies in aerospace, shipbuilding, vehicle manufacturing and steel have been privatised.

The policies have been controversial. Not all economists and politicians agree on their benefits, invariably claiming that a new type of monopoly has often emerged. A particularly controversial privatisation has been that of the rail network. Critics argue that this is a 'privatisation too far' and that the natural monopoly argument favours public ownership and not privatisation.

Improve your answer

Read the question and answer below and see how you can improve it using the suggestions that follow.

Question

a *Analyse what is meant by a contestable market.* **[12]**

b *For a market of your choice, discuss the extent to which this market is contestable.* **[13]**

a A market is a place where buyers and sellers of a product get together for trade. With no government intervention, prices are determined in the market by the combined forces of demand and supply. If suppliers exert control in the market, then they can influence prices and the market is not particularly competitive. This is where the idea of a contestable market fits in.

The name suggests that sellers can compete fairly with each other. Unlike monopoly and perfect competition, a contestable market is not really a market structure. It is more concerned with a set of conditions that occur in a market.

These conditions include the opportunity for new firms to enter a market. Even if they do not enter a market, the point is that they are there, waiting in the wings as it were for an opportunity to move into the market. If an established firm is making profits, then this is a sign that a new firm should try to enter this market.

b The air transport market in India is one which has recently become more competitive.

This market has only recently experienced deregulation and even then, the deregulation is not complete. There is a restriction which means that only Indian airlines with a minimum number of aircraft can operate freely in the market. The established airlines are Air India and Jet Airways and they have had domestic routes such as Mumbai to Delhi and to small places such as Aurangabad for many years. Deregulation has seen new companies like Spice Jet and Indigo enter the market. Another big firm Kingfisher, owned by the brewery, has gone bust.

The fares charged are low and very competitive. Airlines also compete on the services they provide and on customer service like free snacks for passengers. The rapid growth of new services has put a lot of pressure on the main hub airports such as Delhi, Kolkota and Mumbai. There is a brand new airport here.

Suggestions on how to improve this answer

Part (a):

This answer has a reasonable opening and makes some valid points but lacks effective **analysis** of the characteristics of a contestable market. More specifically:

- Free entry, an essential feature, is only hinted at in the third paragraph. Elaboration is required.

- The reference to profits is too vague.

- It could say that a contestable market can apply even in a monopoly or in an oligopoly.

- A very good answer would refer to the need to have regulations to ensure fair competition.

Part (b):

This is very good in terms of factual detail but needs to be expanded.

- The main requirement is to refer back to the characteristics of a contestable market identified in part (a) and to **discuss** the extent to which they are evidenced in the Indian domestic air transport market

- Following from this, it is necessary to conclude by saying whether the market really is contestable. The second paragraph makes a valid point about a local restriction on domestic airlines; this should be an essential part of the conclusion.

Learning outcomes

The exercises in this chapter will help you to practise what you have learnt about:

- why an efficient allocation of resources is desirable
- what is meant by deadweight loss
- how fiscal policies can be used to correct market failure where there are production and consumption externalities
- how a range of other policies can also be used to correct market failure
- what is meant by equity and analysing how governments can use various policies to redistribute income and wealth
- how labour markets operate and why government intervention is invariably necessary
- the effectiveness of government microeconomic intervention.

KEY TERMS

You should **know and understand** what is meant by the following key terms. These terms are defined in Chapter 8 of the course book.

Deadweight loss	**Universal benefits**
Regulations	**Progressive tax**
Pollution permits	**Regressive tax**
Property rights	**Negative income tax**
Privatisation	**Intergenerational equity**
Equity	**Derived demand**
Wealth	**Marginal revenue product**
Lorenz curve	**Transfer earnings**
Gini coefficient	**Economic rent**
Means-tested benefits	**Monopsony**
Poverty trap	**Government failure**

Exercises

1 In March 2016, in its annual Union budget, the Indian government announced an increase in Aviation Turbine fuel duty from 8 to 14%.

   i Show this increase on Figure 8.1.

   ii Shade in the area of 'deadweight' loss and say what it means.

   iii Make a few notes on whether you feel that this increase in duty will lead to an increase in air fares and a reduction in the number of people travelling by air. Justify your answers.

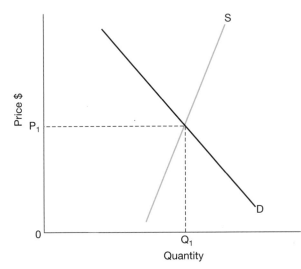

Figure 8.1 Fuel duty increase

2 In order to achieve a more efficient allocation of resources, a range of policies has been suggested to correct the market failure arising from negative externalities.

For the two negative externalities shown (air pollution and illegal waste disposal), think about which of the policies shown might be effective and some of the problems there might be when the policy is implemented. Then complete the table below.

i Problem: Atmospheric pollution from factories:

Policy	Likely effectiveness	Problems
Indirect tax		
Subsidy		
Information provision		
Pollution permits		
Property rights		
Licences		
'Nudge' principles		

ii Problem: Illegal dumping of waste:

Policy	Likely effectiveness	Problems
Indirect tax		
Subsidy		
Information provision		
Pollution permits		
Property rights		
Licences		
'Nudge' principles		

3 i In 2015, Malaysia's prime minister stated that the government wanted to see 'a more equal society' amidst growing concerns about income inequality.

In 2002, the Gini coefficient after taxes and transfers was 0.46. In 2014, it was 0.41.

On the basis of the above evidence, are growing concerns about income inequality justified? Explain your response.

ii Consider the bar charts in Figure 8.2.

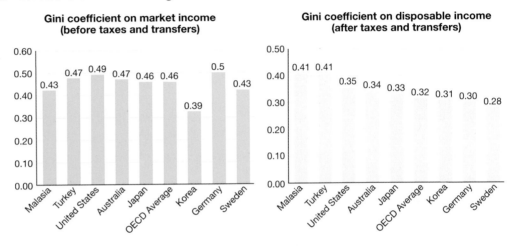

Figure 8.2 How to narrow the gap between rich and poor in Malaysia

a Looking at the fall in the Gini coefficients after taxes and transfers have been taken into account, which country experienced:

– the smallest Gini coefficient?

– the largest Gini coefficient?

b What factors are likely to determine the difference between the two Gini coefficients shown in the bar charts?

4 Table 8.1 assumes that a firm is in a perfectly competitive industry in the short run. Labour which costs $40 per worker is the only variable factor of production. The price of the product is $10 per unit.

a Fill in the blank cells

Labour (workers)	Total output	Marginal physical product	Price of product	Marginal revenue product	Wage per worker	Contribution* of each worker
1	5					
2	11					
3	18					
4	22					
5	25					
6	26					
7	26					

Table 8.1

* This is the difference between the value of the marginal revenue product and the wage per worker.

97

b How many workers would you expect the firm to employ?

c Make a few notes on why it is not always possible to estimate the marginal revenue product of a worker.

TIP
It would help set the context of your answer if you could describe the distribution of income in your country and how it has changed in recent years.

5 It has been suggested that improved education, taxation and social policies are the best ways to achieve a more equitable distribution of income.

a Explain how such policies might achieve a more equitable distribution of income. **[A]**

b With reference to your own country, comment on whether a more equitable distribution of income might be achieved by such policies. **[E]**

6 Since 2004, the UK economy has experienced a net migration of almost 1 million workers from Poland.

a Use economic analysis to explain the effects of this migration on the UK labour market and the labour market in Poland. **[A]**

b Discuss whether migration is the best way for counteracting skill shortages in a labour market. **[E]**

TIP
It may help to know that the workforce of the UK is around 34m and that of Poland 19m.

Exam-style questions

Data response question

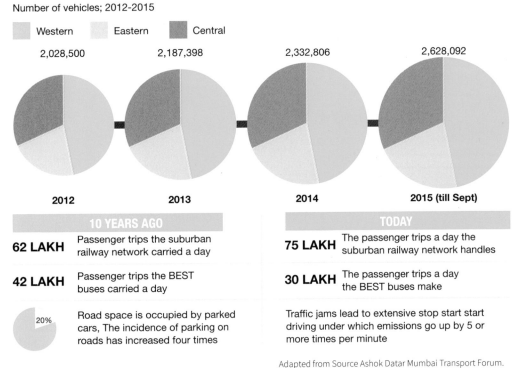

Building more roads – the answer to Mumbai's traffic problems?

Number of vehicles; 2012-2015

- Western
- Eastern
- Central

2,028,500	2,187,398	2,332,806	2,628,092
2012	2013	2014	2015 (till Sept)

10 YEARS AGO		TODAY	
62 LAKH	Passenger trips the suburban railway network carried a day	**75 LAKH**	The passenger trips a day the suburban railway network handles
42 LAKH	Passenger trips the BEST buses carried a day	**30 LAKH**	The passenger trips a day the BEST buses make
20%	Road space is occupied by parked cars, The incidence of parking on roads has increased four times		Traffic jams lead to extensive stop start start driving under which emissions go up by 5 or more times per minute

Adapted from Source Ashok Datar Mumbai Transport Forum.

Figure 8.3 Number of vehicles used in Mumbai 2012–2015

Mumbai, India's largest city with around 13m people, has some of the most serious traffic congestion in the world. This is hardly surprising given that another 295,000 vehicles were added to Mumbai's streets in 2015. Chaos is inevitable as the city planners continue to give priority to private vehicles over public transport.

Most of those who use the roads for their daily commute either have their own cars and two-wheelers or use taxis and the iconic auto-rickshaws. These all fight for space along with trucks, especially in the evening peak period. The western suburbs, which have the most private vehicles, are worst affected.

Congestion resulting from increasing levels of car use tends to be a self-inflicted problem. Philipp Rode from the London School of Economics argues that the increase in vehicles in Mumbai is no different to that in most cities in developing economies – the problem is made worse by the compact nature of Mumbai and its high density of population, which make the city very vulnerable to the increasing flood of vehicles.

The city aims to improve its mobility by building even more new roads and flyovers which, according to local transport planner Priyanka Vasudevan, will only serve to induce more vehicle congestion. In his opinion, 'We need to rethink our approach to congestion and utilise the space that is available more effectively'.

Source: Hindustan Times, 24 February 2016 (adapted).

Notes: LAKH – an Indian word for 100,000; BEST – Brichanmumbai Electric Supply and Transport.

a Describe the changes shown to the pattern of transport in Mumbai. **[3]**

b State and explain **two** possible reasons for the increase in the number of vehicles in 2015 **[4]**

> **REMEMBER**
>
> This is a typical question containing data and text. 'Scan' the data and pick out the main issues in the text. Note the mark allocations.

99

c Use economic analysis to explain why 'congestion resulting from increasing levels of car use tends to be a self-inflicted problem'. [6]

d Discuss whether building new roads is really the best long-term way of improving mobility in Mumbai. [7]

Essay questions

1 The economy of Singapore relies heavily on migrant labour.

  a Explain how an increase in migrant workers is likely to affect wage rates in Singapore. [12]

  b Comment on whether the Singapore government is justified in trying to reduce its demand for migrant labour. [13]

2 Discuss the extent to which market demand and supply factors can be used to explain wage differentials. [25]

3 Governments throughout the world are striving to reduce greenhouse gases yet in Europe, Asia, Africa and the USA, they are pressing ahead with the deregulation of air transport markets.

  a Explain how the increased use of air transport contributes to the problem of climate change. [12]

  b Comment on the extent to which this situation is one of government failure. [13]

4 a Explain the difference between equity and efficiency in income and wealth redistribution. [12]

  b Discuss whether policies to redistribute income and wealth can be both equitable and efficient. [13]

5 Comment on the view that fiscal measures alone cannot satisfactorily correct market failure. [25]

Multiple choice questions

1 The diagram shows an individual's supply of labour curve.

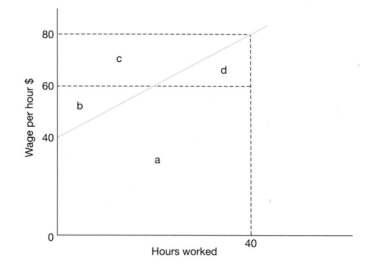

Figure 8.4 Supply of labour curve

The worker is offered a job which is for a 40-hour week.

Which area measures the smallest amount the person would have to be paid to accept the job offer?

A b + c   **B** a + d   **C** a + b   **D** a + b + c + d

2   Which of these government policies is **not** classified as a regulation?

    A   A licence to drive a motor vehicle.

    B   A ban on certain dangerous drugs.

    C   An indirect tax on sugary drinks.

    D   A permit to pollute the environment.

3   Table 8.2 shows recent Gini coefficients for the so-called BRICS economies.

Brazil	0.53
Russia	0.42
India	0.34
China	0.47
South Africa	0.65

Table 8.2 Recent Gini coefficients for the BRICS economies

Which of these statements is correct?

    A   Brazil has a more equal distribution of income than China.

    B   India has the most equal distribution of income.

    C   The distribution of income in Russia is becoming less equal.

    D   South Africa has a high level of income inequality because its GDP per head is the least of all BRICS economies.

4   The so-called 'poverty trap' occurs where:

    A   Only one person in the family is able to work to support the rest.

    B   A family cannot afford to live at a basic subsistence level.

    C   A family is better off on means-tested benefits rather than where those able to work are in employment.

    D   Even with means-tested benefits, a family is unable to afford to live at a basic subsistence level.

5 The diagram below shows the effect on the market equilibrium when a green tax is applied to a polluting chemical company.

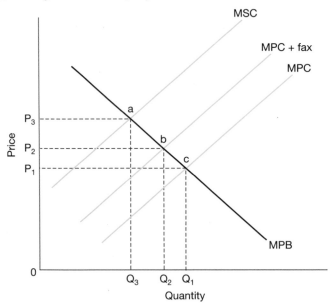

Figure 8.5 The effect on the market equilibrium when a green tax is applied to a polluting chemical company

Which of the following statements is correct?

A The market failure has not been fully corrected by the imposition of a tax.

B The market failure has been corrected by the imposition of a tax.

C The burden of the tax will fall on the producer.

D The burden of the tax will fall on consumers of the firm's products.

Think like an economist

Key economic myth

The purpose of road pricing in the form of an indirect tax on road users is to reduce traffic congestion.

Sorry to disappoint, but this is an economic myth since the true purpose of the indirect tax is to correct market failure. Imposing the indirect tax reduces demand from some road users and hence as a side effect, a fall in the level of traffic congestion.

Key economist

A.C. Pigou was an outstanding welfare economist. The content of his book *The Economics of Welfare* underpins what we now know as a classic market failure, namely where there are externalities in the market – this means that costs imposed or benefits that accrue to others (usually called third parties) are not taken into account by the person taking the action.

Pigou's ideas were rather narrower in scope to those used by contemporary economists. He argued that industrialists were only concerned about their own interests and not the social interest. They consequently had no incentive to internalise what we now call the marginal external cost. On the other hand, individuals who receive a benefit from some third-party action had no incentive to pay for it.

Pigou's solution was simple – impose a tax (known as a Pigovian tax) to discourage activities that produce a negative externality and provide subsidies for activities that give positive externalities.

This approach remains central to government microeconomic intervention and the correction market failure.

Key economic diagram

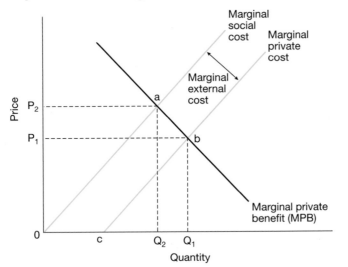

Figure 8.6 Key diagram

Key points:

- Marginal social cost = marginal private cost + marginal external cost.

- Original output is at Q_1 and price P_1.

- A specific (Pigovian) tax equal to the marginal external cost results in a reduced output of Q_2 and an increased price of P_2. This outcome fully corrects the market failure.

- The total taxes paid is equal to the area Oabc.

- If the indirect tax paid is less than the marginal external cost, then government intervention is not fully correcting the market failure.

- The value of the marginal external cost is very difficult to estimate.

Key economic issue

Markets increasingly fail to provide the best allocation of resources. One of the most common examples is the case of traffic congestion which affects virtually all towns and cities in developed and developing economies alike.

To the economist, the problem of market failure is because some road users are paying too much and others not paying enough for their use of the road network. This is shown on the key diagram through marginal social cost being greater than marginal private cost. As a consequence, there is a misallocation of resources due to the cost of various negative externalities including:

- increased running costs (private costs) for many road users

- increased journey times

- reduced efficiency of buses that use the road network

- increased strain and stress for all road users

- increased greenhouse gas emissions due to slow moving traffic.

Various ways have been tried to combat this problem including:

- building more roads to increase capacity

- improving and subsidising public transport

- developing new mass transit systems

- taxing fuel and the ownership of vehicles

- physically restricting vehicle use.

Arguably, all have failed in their own ways because they do not tackle head on the real issue, that of market failure.

Key economic policy

Economists do not often agree, but one policy that most would like to see introduced to combat congestion is what is known as 'road pricing'.

Road pricing is where a direct charge is made for using road space. Ideally, it is a charge that depends on when and where a vehicle is used and on the volume of traffic. As a charge, it is best applied where there is a certain degree of accuracy in its measurement. Advances in technology are such that this is now a distinct possibility.

The only real example that approaches this ideal is the ERP system in Singapore. Drivers entering a central area zone are required to pay a variable charge depending on the time of day and traffic levels. The system is fastidiously monitored, with fines for non-compliance.

The congestion charge in London has operated since 2002. It is a flat rate charge for access into a central zone at peak periods. It is a complex system in terms of its operation due to the many exemptions that have to be applied. Less sophisticated zonal charging systems are applied in cities in Norway and Sweden, whilst other major cities are seriously considering introducing similar charges.

Improve your answer

Read the question and answer below and see how you can improve it using the suggestions that follow.

Question

Combatting the effects of climate change is one of the most pressing problems facing the global economy. Using examples of your choice, discuss the likely effectiveness of policies that are designed to reduce CO_2 emissions. **[25]**

There is growing concern about the effects of climate change on the global economy. If what scientists say is correct, then increasing CO_2 emissions are already the cause of climate change. This is leading to increasing temperatures and extreme weather conditions with flooding and tsunami's having devastating effects. Think of Japan, the Philippines and the USA.

The increase in CO_2 emissions comes from the demands of the world's increasing population. The growth of air travel, the increasing number of cars (6m more per year in China alone) and the use of coal-fired power stations release more and more CO_2 in the atmosphere. We need air travel and cars but it is difficult to know what we can do to reduce their environmental impact. A fix for power stations would be to make them nuclear or solar powered.

Here, we have a situation of negative externalities. Look at flying. People who travel by plane do not think about the damage they are doing to others and to the environment. This is so in my own country, India, where there has been a big increase in the number of domestic airline routes.

One way that could help is to put a tax on air travel. This has been done in England. The tax is called Air ???? and is paid for on top of the price of airline tickets. It was introduced many years ago to try to cut down on the demand for flying. It does not appear to have been successful as London's Heathrow airport has no spare capacity for any more flights.

Another way is to control the emissions from aircraft. This is a technical regulation and is there to improve the use of fuel in older aircraft. It is a similar idea to how vehicle manufactures are required to fit catalytic converters to many cars. This has not been effective as the VW scandal indicates.

Suggestions on how to improve this answer

- The answer starts off well and has some interesting examples *but* does it really address the point of the question?
- It is also very short for an answer to a 25-mark question.
- How might you incorporate more economic analysis? This is the biggest weakness.
- What diagrams could you incorporate?
- What other examples might you include as well as flying?
- Only include facts if you know they are correct (Air *Passenger Duty*).
- Avoid spurious deductions, e.g. Heathrow airport is at full capacity because Air ???? is not working.
- What approach should you take in the final paragraph? There is no conclusion in this answer.

Learning outcomes

The exercises in this chapter will help you to practise what you have learnt about:

- economic growth, economic development and sustainability, the factors that contribute to economic growth and the costs and benefits of growth
- how national income statistics are used as measures of economic growth and living standards; other monetary and non-monetary indicators of living standards and economic development
- the characteristics of developed, developing and emerging (BRICS) economies: by population growth and structure, employment composition, external trade and urbanisation and how economic growth rates and living standards are compared over time and between countries
- what influences the size and components of the labour force; labour productivity; the distinction between full employment and the natural rate of unemployment
- the causes and consequences of unemployment, types of unemployment, the unemployment rate and why there are difficulties in measuring unemployment
- policies to correct unemployment
- the circular flow of income, the multiplier and the average and marginal propensities to save and consume
- inflationary and deflationary gaps, the full employment level of income and the equilibrium level of income
- the difference between autonomous and induced investment; the accelerator
- the Quantity Theory of Money and the sources of money supply in an open economy
- the difference between the Keynesian and monetarist approaches in theory; liquidity preference theory
- the types of aid, the nature of dependency and the role of trade and investment, multinationals and foreign direct investment (FDI) in promoting growth
- the impact of external debt and the role of the IMF and the World Bank.

KEY TERMS

You should **know and understand** what is meant by the following key terms. These terms are defined in Chapter 9 of the course book.

Economic growth	Measurable Economic Welfare	Optimum population
Economic development	Human Development Index	Prebisch-Singer hypothesis
Sustainable development	Multidimensional Poverty Index	Labour productivity
Actual economic growth	Kuznets curve	Unemployment
Potential economic growth	Developed economy	Full employment
Output gap	Developing economy	Natural rate of unemployment
Negative output gap	Poverty cycles	Frictional unemployment
Positive output gap	Development traps	Structural unemployment
Trade cycle	Emerging economies	Cyclical unemployment
National income	World Bank	Claimant count
Gross national income	Primary sector	Labour force survey
Money GDP	Secondary sector	Reflationary fiscal or monetary policy measures
Real GDP	Tertiary sector	
Shadow economy	Quaternary sector	Multiplier
Purchasing power parity	Malthusian theory	Open economy
National debt	Dependency ratio	Closed economy

Circular flow of income

Marginal propensity to save

Marginal rate of taxation

Marginal propensity to import

Aggregate expenditure

Consumption

Disposable income

Average propensity to consume

Dissaving

Saving

Marginal propensity to consume

Consumption function

Saving function

Average propensity to save

Investment

Government spending

Net exports

Injections

Withdrawals

Paradox of thrift

Inflationary gap

Deflationary gap

Autonomous investment

Induced investment

Accelerator theory

Capital-output ratio

Quantity Theory of Money

Fisher equation

Narrow money

Broad money

Credit multiplier

Liquidity ratio

Government securities

Quantitative easing

Total currency flow

Keynesians

Monetarists

Liquidity preference

Transactions motive

Precautionary motive

Active balances

Speculative motive

Idle balances

Liquidity trap

Foreign aid

Dependence

International Monetary Fund

Virtuous cycle

Foreign direct investment

Exercises

1 Actual economic growth occurs in the short run when output increases. Potential economic growth is long run and comes about when there is an increase in the economy's productive potential.

    a Draw production possibility diagrams to show each of these two types of economic growth.

    b Consider the following situations. For each, say whether it is actual or potential economic growth:

        i A decrease in unemployment

        ii An increase in the proportion of women in the labour force.

        iii A shift outwards of an economy's production possibility curve.

        iv A movement along an economy's production possibility curve.

        v A new technological invention that increases productivity.

        vi Improved utilisation of existing capital assets.

2

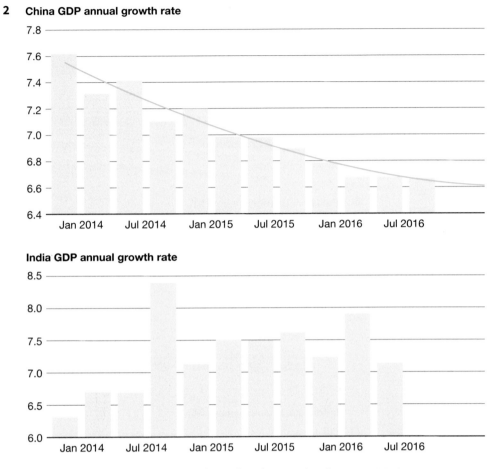

Figure 9.1 Annual growth rates of GDP for China and India, 2014–2016

a Compare the annual growth rates in GDP for China and India from January 2014 to July 2016.

b Give some possible reasons for the differences.

3 Table 9.1 shows two different measures of GDP per head for China and for India in 2015.

	GDP per head ($US)	GDP per head ($US, PPP)[1]
China	6,420	13,400
India	1,805	5,730

[1] Purchasing power parity.

Table 9.1 GDP per head for China and for India in 2015

a What is the difference between the two measures?

b Compare the two measures for each country. Give some possible reasons for the differences you have observed.

4 In 2015, the GDP per head of Malaysia was at an all-time high of US$10,876, an increase of US$360 on 2014.

Make a few notes on whether this increase means an improvement in living standards for the people of Malaysia.

109

5 There are three main types of unemployment: frictional, structural and cyclical. Below are some reasons for unemployment. Say which type most closely matches each reason:

a Unemployment resulting from garment manufacturing moving from the UK to Bangladesh.

b A global downturn following the 2008 financial crisis in the USA.

c People out of work before starting a new job.

d People who are unable to work due to illness or a physical handicap.

e Falling aggregate demand due to the need to reduce the level of inflation.

f Unemployment amongst banana pickers during the growing season.

6 Pakistan: Unemployment (%)

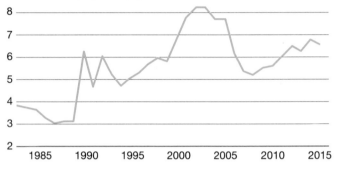

Indonesia: Unemployment (%)

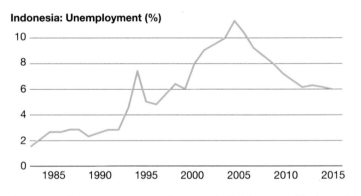

Figure 9.2 Percentage unemployment in Pakistan and Indonesia

a Compare the unemployment rates for Pakistan and Indonesia over the period 1980–2015.

b What evidence is there that unemployment in each country was affected by:

i The Asian financial crisis of the mid-1990s?

ii The US financial crisis of 2008–2012?

7 Figure 9.3 shows an economy with an initial aggregate demand function of AD and two other aggregate demand functions AD_1 and AD_2.

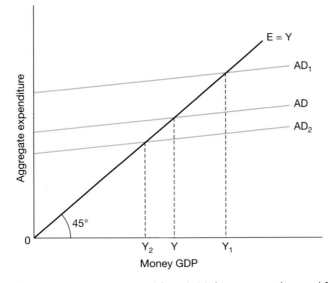

Figure 9.3 An economy with an initial aggregate demand function of AD and two other aggregate demand functions AD_1 and AD_2

a What is the initial equilibrium level of income?

b If the marginal propensity to consume increases, which is the new aggregate demand function and equilibrium level of income?

c Use Figure 9.3 to describe how a fall in government spending will affect the initial equilibrium position.

8 Figure 9.4 shows how according to Keynes, the rate of interest is determined.

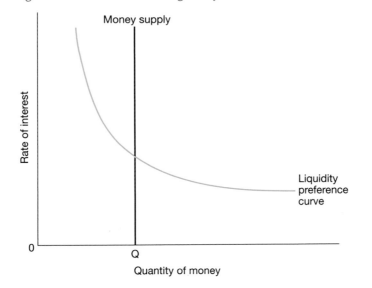

Figure 9.4 How the rate of interest is determined, according to Keynes

a On Figure 9.4:

    i Show how an increase in the money supply affects the rate of interest.

    ii Show how a decrease in the money supply affects the rate of interest.

b For each of the above, say why the change in the money supply is likely to be required and how this is expected to affect aggregate demand.

9 The estimated value of the multiplier in China is 2.6; in the UK it is 1.3.

    a Account for the difference in the two estimates. [Ap]

    b Suppose China and the UK each decide to build a new nuclear power station costing US$100m. Using the multiplier estimates, analyse the contrasting impacts on GDP. [A]

10 a Explain how quantitative easing affects the money supply in an economy. [A]

    b Comment on why quantitative easing may not necessarily always achieve its objectives. [E]

11 a Analyse why many developing countries are faced with serious problems of external debt. [A]

    b Discuss whether the world's most developed economies could do more to relieve the debt problems faced by many developing countries. [E]

TIP
Think about leakages.

TIP
A good answer should make reference to countries that have tried quantitative easing.

Exam-style questions

Data response questions

Global contrasts in fertility rates

Sustained economic growth can be achieved through an increase in potential output. This can come from an increase in the quantity and quality of resources available. One such resource is a country's population.

The characteristics of a developing economy's population can be shown in various ways. One such way is that high fertility rates contribute to an increase in population; in contrast, fertility rates in most developed economies are lower and are responsible in some cases for a declining population.

It is estimated that the replacement fertility rate that is necessary for a stable population is around 2.0 in industrial countries, rising to 2.5 to 3.3 for most developing economies. An exception to this norm is China where a low fertility rate is increasingly alarming to the government.

Table 9.2 shows the estimated fertility rates for selected economies in 2015.

Nigeria	5.19	UK	1.89
Sierra Leone	4.80	USA	1.87
Central African Republic	4.41	Russia	1.61
Pakistan	2.75	PR China	1.60
Malaysia	2.55	Germany	1.44
India	2.48	Italy	1.43
Bangladesh	2.40	Hong Kong	1.18
Indonesia	2.15	Singapore	0.81

*Note: This refers to the average number of children that would be born per woman if all women lived to the end of their childbearing years.

Source: World Fact Book, CIA, 2016.

Table 9.2 Total fertility rates*, 2015 (estimated)

1 a Other than fertility rates, state **two** other population indicators you could use to describe a developing economy. **[2]**

 b Explain two likely reasons for a fall in fertility rates in some developed economies such as the USA and Italy. **[4]**

 c Analyse the likely economic effects of high fertility rates in developing economies such as Nigeria and Sierra Leone. **[4]**

 d The economies of Hong Kong and Singapore continue to grow despite low fertility rates. How might you explain this? **[4]**

 e Comment on why a low fertility rate is 'alarming' for the Chinese government. **[6]**

113

What else can be done to stimulate Japan's ailing economy?

Japan's economy is the third largest in the world after the United States and China, yet for many years, the performance of the macroeconomy has defied what might have been expected from accepted economic theory. Growth has stuttered from periods of low growth in GDP to periods of recession; consumer prices have fallen as have wages. Barely positive, and now negative, interest rates have failed to stimulate consumer spending. Finally, years of quantitative easing have also failed and resulted in Japan having the heaviest public debt in the world.

In 2012, Prime Minister Shinzo Abe won power on a promise to rekindle economic growth and reducing the public-sector deficit. Until now, implementing this policy has been largely left to the central bank's monetary policies. In a change of direction, it is reported that Mr Abe's government is putting together a package of spending measures worth ¥28 trillion. A planned increase in the national sales tax has been postponed.

To many economists, this U-turn appears to be acknowledging the limits of its monetary policy tools. Some have argued that as an extreme measure, the central bank should inject 'helicopter money' into the economy. This is a term that involves dumping cash straight into the economy by giving it to consumers or directly financing government spending. Central bankers have long viewed such a policy as dangerous (think of Zimbabwe), but some specialists say that Japan is now running out of options.

Source: Japan resists strong medicine, *International New York Times*, 30/31 July 2016.

2 **a** Explain what is meant by quantitative easing and why it has been applied to the Japanese economy. **[4]**

  b Using a diagram, explain why according to economic theory, low interest rates should stimulate an economy. **[4]**

  c What evidence is there to suggest that the Japanese economy is in the 'liquidity trap'? **[4]**

  d Using the information in the last two paragraphs, discuss whether the proposed new policies might stimulate growth in Japan's economy. **[8]**

Essay questions

1 Imagine you have been asked to produce a report about the quality of life in your country. Discuss what would be important to include in your report and what economic indicators you would use in order to reach a conclusion. **[25]**

Cambridge International AS and A Level Economics 9708 Paper 42 Q6 May/June 2016.

2 **a** Assess how changes in interest rates might influence investment. **[12]**

  b Some economists argue that increases in investment cause national income to increase. Others argue that the reverse is true: an increase in national income brings about investment.

  Discuss whether both these seemingly contradictory statements can be true. **[13]**

Cambridge International AS and A Level Economics 9708 Paper 42 Q6 Feb/March 2016.

3 In 2015, China's economy grew by no more than 8%, a significant decrease on previous years when double-digit growth was recorded.

  Discuss the possible effects of this reduction on the Chinese economy and the economies of its trading partners. **[25]**

TIP

Think carefully about this question. There is a danger that you will write a long descriptive answer. So, consider your own country and what is really important; include only those indicators that are important.

4   a   Explain what is mean by inflationary and deflationary gaps. [12]

    b   Comment on the view that 'inflationary and deflationary gaps are different and therefore require different policies to close them'. [13]

5   a   Explain the main causes of unemployment in your country. [12]

    b   Discuss whether unemployment in your country is best reduced using supply-side policies. [13]

6   a   Explain what is meant by sustainable development. [12]

    b   Discuss the ways in which economic development in your country might become more sustainable. [13]

7   In September 2016, official interest rates in Japan, Sweden and Switzerland were all negative at –0.1%, –0.5% and –0.75% respectively.

    Explain what these rates mean and discuss why they have been thought necessary. [25]

Multiple choice questions

1   A developing country receives foreign aid from a more developed country in order to boost its long-run economic growth. Which of the following is likely to be the best way for the developing economy to spend this money to meet its objective?

    A   Increase the subsidies paid to farmers to produce more products for export.

    B   Clean up polluted land.

    C   Abolish income tax for the lowest paid workers.

    D   Improve electricity and water supplies.

2   The consumption function C for an economy with no government sector and no foreign trade is:

    $C = \$2{,}000 + 0.8Y$

    Assume an initial income (Y) of $1,000

    If income (Y) increases by $500, what will be the new level of consumption?

    A $2,500

    B $3,500

    C $3,200

    D   None of these.

3   The government in an economy is undecided as to whether it should increase its own spending on roads by $50m or reduce direct taxes by $50m. It has been advised that building new roads will have a bigger effect on aggregate demand. Why is this?

    A   All of the $50m spent on roads is added to aggregate demand.

    B   A reduction in direct taxes takes a long time to have an impact.

    C   The multiplier for road expenditure is small.

    D   Not all of the increased income from reduced taxation will be spent or consumption.

4 Figure 9.5 shows how the rate of interest is determined in an economy. L is the demand for money and MS is the supply of money.

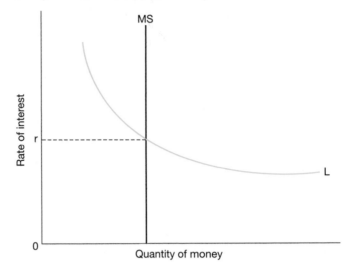

Figure 9.5 How the rate of interest is determined in an economy

If the supply of money is reduced, which of these statements is correct?

A The rate of interest will rise.

B The rate of interest will fall.

C The rate of interest will remain the same.

D It is not possible to tell.

5 Which of these statements is most consistent with the Keynesian view of the role of government in the economy?

A The government should use a budget deficit where there is high unemployment.

B The government should not interfere even if there is high unemployment.

C The government should increase the money supply to increase employment.

D The government's priority should be to keep a low rate of inflation.

Think like an economist

Key economic myth

Low interest rates provide a monetary stimulus whereby firms increase their investments and consumers spend more

Prior to the financial crisis in 2008, most economists, Keynesian and Monetarists, would have agreed that this was true. The reality is that interest rates have been drastically cut to record low levels such as the UK's 0.25% rate announced in August 2016 and yet banks are struggling to lend money, firms are cautious about investing in new equipment and consumers are reluctant to spend even though the returns on savings are negligible.

What is going on? It appears to contradict much of economic theory.

Key economists

The choice of economists for this chapter is obvious, given their impact on macroeconomic theory and its application to government economic policies.

John Maynard Keynes, a Cambridge economist, was so influential that a whole branch of economics (Keynesian economics) has been attributed to him. His ideas at the time were revolutionary and contrary to what was the norm. Traditional government policy was for a balanced budget whereby income from taxation matched government spending. At a time of serious depression in the British and global economy, Keynes was highly critical of this approach in his *General Theory of Employment Interest and Money*.

Keynes developed the concept of aggregate demand. He maintained that the high unemployment at the time could only be reduced with the help of substantial government spending. This would increase aggregate demand, create jobs for the unemployed and generate increases in consumption and investment. His ideas also took hold in the USA where the federal government embarked on a series of public works projects to get the unemployed back into work.

Keynes' theories and principles have been reviewed, revised and developed by many UK and US economists and have been the bedrock of economic policies. However, they have been heavily criticised by monetary economists, notably Milton Friedman (see below), so much so that government economic policies have become predominantly monetarist. It is very significant at a time of global recession and uncertainty, Keynes' approach is gradually coming back into favour.

Milton Friedman, a Chicago economist, was once called 'the most influential economist of the second half of the twentieth century' by the *Economist* newspaper. He was a strong critic of Keynes and rejected Keynsian principles on the grounds that they led to 'stagflation', whereby stagnation and inflation occurred simultaneously.

Friedman's alternative approach was that of Monetarism. Central to this is that changes in the money supply are responsible for periods of fluctuation in the macroeconomy. At a time of high inflation such as during the 1970s, Friedman maintained that there was a clear relationship between inflation and the money supply. To control inflation, there should be proper control of the money supply in the economy.

Friedman rejected the then prevailing view that high inflation was caused by cost-push factors such as rising oil prices and wage settlements. He rejected the use of fiscal policy as a tool of demand management, arguing that governments should only intervene in the workings of the free market mechanism when absolutely necessary. He was also a strong supporter of privatisation and deregulation and for exchange rates to be allowed to freely float in the foreign exchange market.

It is significant that Friedman's monetarist ideas have been applied by successive governments especially in the UK and USA since the early 1980s.

Key economic diagrams

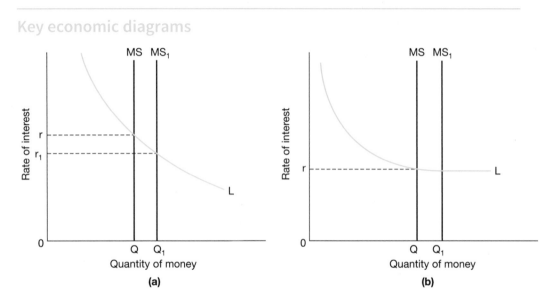

Figure 9.6 Key diagrams

Key points:

a ▪ r is the equilibrium rate of interest where the supply of money MS is equal to the demand for money L.

▪ An increase in the supply of money from banks reduces the interest rate to r.

▪ More bonds are demanded, bidding up their price.

▪ The demand for money now increases until a new equilibrium rate of interest, r, is reached.

b ▪ An increase in the money supply from MS to MS_1 has no effect on the rate of interest.

▪ Holding bonds is no longer attractive.

▪ The increase in money supply has no effect on the rate of interest (liquidity trap).

Key economic issue

Monetary policy has historically used two main approaches, interest rates and the money supply. If an economy is facing recession, the obvious thing to do is to cut interest rates and increase the supply of money. These measures provide an incentive for businesses to increase their capital investment and for consumers to borrow more money to fund increased consumption. In this way, aggregate demand increases, more jobs are created and recession is likely to be avoided.

So, why is it that since 2009, with interest rates in the UK at 0.5% (0.25% since August 2016) the macroeconomy has been struggling to avoid recession? The simple answer to a complex situation is that business confidence is weak, consumers are holding back on their expenditure and commercial banks seem to want to keep hold of their funds. More specifically, in the UK, in 2016 there was uncertainty over the Brexit result and its impact on short- and long-term economic prospects. These are not factors that can be taken into account by the traditional economic theory.

Key economic policy

It is in the above context that quantitative easing has been applied as a new form of monetary policy especially in the UK but also in the USA, Japan, Australia and the Euro area.

Adopting quantitative easing recognises that low interest rates are not being effective. Central banks use quantitative easing to directly pump money into the financial system in contrast to reducing interest rates which is an indirect method.

The central bank buys government bonds in order to create money. In turn, this is used to buy bonds from banks and pension funds. This increases the amount of useable funds that financial institutions have to lend to businesses and individual consumers. It could even lead to lower interest rates, giving a further boost to the economy.

Quantitative easing is not without risks, the biggest of which is that pumping more money into the economy could lead to higher inflation. Where inflation is not a concern, then quantitative easing is likely to be well received.

Review your answers

Below are two typical questions drawn from the content of this chapter. Try to answer them as best you can and then review your answers.

1 The BRICS countries are often referred to as 'emerging' economies.

   a Explain what indicators you might use to describe the characteristics of an 'emerging' economy. **[12]**

   b Comment upon the policies that are most likely to be put in place to increase their level of economic development. **[13]**

2 **a** Contrast the Keynesian and Monetarist approaches to managing the macroeconomy. **[12]**

   b With reference to your own country, assess which of these approaches is most suited to managing the economy. **[13]**

Advice on how to answer this question

1 a Try to select only those indicators that are most indicative of emerging economies:

- Focus on those that can show recent annual rates of change such as GDP, GDP per head, economic structure, exports to developed economies.

- Improvements in education, health and IT could also be used.

- Do not feel you have to include indicators that are more specifically used to describe less developed economies.

- Maybe compare with developed economies.

b Various possibilities including:

- Attracting FDI.

- Export-led growth.

- Government and private sector infrastructure development.

- Combatting corruption and the informal economy.

2 a Key differences you should recognise are:

- Keynsian approach focusses on government intervention to manage aggregate demand; maintaining high employment is the prime policy objective.

- Monetarist approach concentrates on the control of inflation through the money supply.

- Deflationary/inflationary gap diagrams and reference to the Quantity Theory of Money will further enhance your answer.

b Make sure your answer applies what you have referred to in part **(a)**. Consider your country's economic priorities (control of inflation? creating more jobs? both?) and then say which approach has prevailed. Or maybe a combination.

(A Level)

Learning outcomes

The exercises in this chapter will help you to practise what you have learnt about:

- the aims of government macroeconomic policy
- the relationship between the internal and external value of money
- the relationship between the balance of payments and inflation
- the possible trade-off between inflation and unemployment
- the Phillips curve and the expectations-augmented Phillips curve
- the problems arising from conflicts between policy objectives
- the existence of government failure in macroeconomic policies
- how the Laffer curve illustrates the possible relationship between tax rates and tax revenue.

You should **know and understand** what is meant by the following key terms. These terms are defined in Chapter 10 of the course book.

Inflation target

Phillips curve

Expectations-augmented Phillips curve

Tinbergen's rule

Government macroeconomic failure

Counter-cyclically

Laffer curve

> **REMEMBER**
> This second macro section builds upon the content in Chapter 9. Note how the learning outcomes focus on analysis and evaluation skills.

Exercises

1   You have now almost completed your A Level economics course. Well done so far. Think about your own economy and its macroeconomic aims by completing the table below.

Macroeconomic aim	Current position	Is this aim achievable?
Low inflation.		
Low unemployment.		
Balance of payments.		
Current account equilibrium.		
Stable exchange rate.		
Sustainable economic growth.		

2 Your answers to Question 1 will no doubt have raised various conflicts between the macroeconomic aims that are shown. Now consider some of these by completing this next table.

Macroeconomic problem	What to do about it	Conflicts with other aims
Inflation is too high.		
Unemployment is too high.		
Current account in persistent deficit.		
Fluctuating exchange rate.		
Low rate of economic growth.		

3 In May 2016, it was reported that Venezuela had an estimated inflation rate of 500% and that this was forecast to rise to 1,500% in 2017.

   a Analyse the likely effects of this hyperinflation on the economy of Venezuela. **[A]**

   b The government is 'desperately trying to reduce imports' as a way of controlling the hyperinflation. Comment upon whether this really is the best policy to pursue. **[E]**

4 The heading and picture in Figure 10.1 are based on those used on the front page of the Times in India on 1 March 2016.

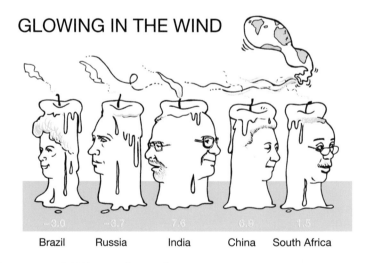

GLOWING IN THE WIND

−3.0	−3.7	7.6	6.9	1.5
Brazil	Russia	India	China	South Africa

Figure 10.1 BRICS growth rates in 2016

   a Analyse the likely effects on the BRICs economies of the different rates of growth achieved in 2015. **[A]**

   b Discuss the policies that India might use to ensure that it continues to 'glow in the wind.' **[E]**

Exam-style questions

Data response questions

China's economic growth falls to lowest in 5 years

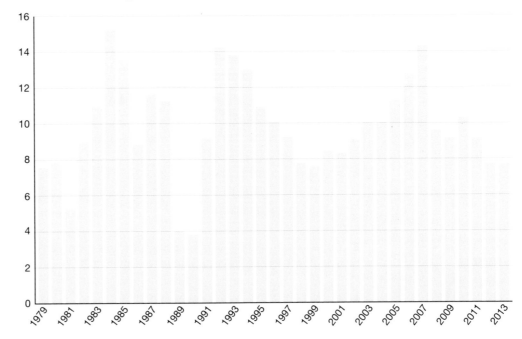

Figure 10.2 Chinese real GDP growth 1979–2013

In October 2014, it was reported that China's economic growth had fallen to a five year low of 7.3%, significantly less than the double-digit growth recorded in some earlier years (see above chart). This rate of growth was still way above that of the USA and EU member states and was seen by some as a welcome re-balancing of the economy.

The slowing in China's growth rate raised new concerns about its damaging impact on the US economy and commodity producers such as Australia, Indonesia and Brazil, all of which are heavily reliant on trade with China.

These concerns are not entirely shared by the Chinese government that is struggling to deal with the debt from its high investment policy arising from the 2009 global recession. China's leaders are seeking to re-focus the economy to growth based on domestic consumption instead of an over-reliance on trade and investment in infrastructure. This revised approach though is not without risks.

China's rapid economic growth has generated other problems, the most serious of which is the issue of air pollution. The authorities have found this difficult to control due to rising traffic levels in cities such as Beijing, Shanghai and Wuhan and the ever-increasing emissions from industrial sites and coal-fired power stations. Some commentators believe that economic growth is the only solution to China's pollution problems. The current and projected slowing of growth must cast serious doubts on this perspective.

Source: The Guardian, 21 October, 2014.

a Describe the trend in China's economic growth since 2,000. **[3]**

b Explain the effects of reduced growth on the Chinese economy and the global economy. **[6]**

c Analyse how China is seeking to alter the factors that contribute to its economic growth. **[5]**

d Discuss whether economic growth is the best way for reducing China's pollution problem. **[6]**

Essay questions

1 'The free market is not the way to achieve a sustainable, efficient use of economic resources. Even the famous economist Adam Smith recognised that there was a need for some government involvement.'

Discuss whether government involvement in the economy might overcome the weaknesses of the free market system. **[25]**

Cambridge International AS and A Level Economics, 9708 Paper 42, Q7 May/June 2015.

2 Following the referendum to withdraw from the EU, the value of the pound quickly depreciated by around 15% against the US dollar and the euro.

Consider whether the UK government should be concerned about this depreciation. **[25]**

3 Comment on how a government might be able to sustain a macroeconomic policy that simultaneously promotes low unemployment and low inflation. **[25]**

4 a With the aid of examples, explain what is meant by macroeconomic government failure. **[12]**

b The UK government will require all employers to pay a 'living wage' from 2017. This will be significantly higher than the current minimum wage.

Discuss how government failure might apply when the 'living wage' is implemented. **[13]**

> **REMEMBER**
> Economic theory disputes that this can be achieved.

124

Multiple choice questions

1 Which of these government policies would be unlikely to reduce poverty?

A An increase in the income tax threshold.

B The introduction of a minimum wage.

C A fall in the price of flat-screen televisions.

D An increase in child benefit payments.

2 The table below gives an economy's unemployment rate and inflation rate for a five-year period.

Year	Unemployment rate %	Inflation rate %
2012	8.2	3.1
2013	6.9	2.8
2014	6.3	3.0
2015	6.6	3.2
2016	6.2	3.2

Table 10.1 Unemployment rate and inflation rate for a five-year period

Which change between consecutive years is consistent with the underlying concept of the Phillips curve?

A 2012–2013 **B** 2013–2014 **C** 2014–2015 **D** 2015–2016

3 Table 10.2 shows how a change in the external value of a currency affects the internal purchasing power of money.

	Change in external value	Change in internal value
A	fall	rise
B	fall	fall
C	rise	fall
D	rise	no change

Table 10.2 How a change in the external value of a currency affects the internal purchasing power of money

Which is correct?

4 Figure 10.3 shows a Laffer Curve.

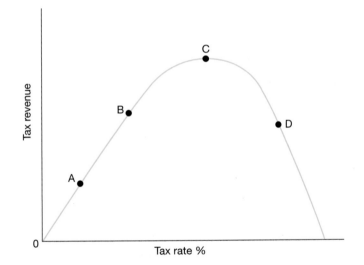

Figure 10.3 Laffer Curve

At which point on the curve are workers most likely to reduce their work effort?

5 The government decides to spend $100m to build a new motorway in an attempt to reduce unemployment. Which of the following is a likely case of government failure?

A The government underestimates the value of the multiplier.

B The government overestimates the value of the multiplier.

C The cost of the new motorway is $80m.

D Not possible to tell from the information provided.

Think like an economist

Key economic myth

Governments should know what policies to use in pursuit of their macroeconomic aims and what the outcomes of such policies should be.

You might think that with an army of economists and a mass of data, governments should know how to meet their macroeconomic objectives. Nothing could be further from the truth. The reality is that macroeconomic problems are not discrete. Conflicts arise in meeting aims and in deciding what policies are going to be most effective. There is the additional problem of unforeseen exogenous shocks to the economy, such as the financial collapse in 2008 that fuelled a global recession.

Key economist

J.K. Galbraith, the Canadian-born economist, was arguably the most well-known American economist of the 20th century. He was controversial through his support of post-Keynesian economics at a time when monetarism and supply-side policies were largely the order of the day. He was also controversial in the way that he made economics relevant to the many political crises that faced the US economy.

Galbraith's 'Affluent Society' was heavily criticised by Milton Friedman amongst others. Their objections were that Galbraith oversimplified economic problems in believing that the free market mechanism was a stumbling block to achieving what reformers wanted to make for a better society. He firmly maintained that 'counterveiling power', including government regulation, was necessary to offset the power of big business and its effects on markets and the economy. Galbraith was also heavily critical of monetary policy arguing that 'complexity was used to disguise or evade the truth; hence his clear support for a post-Keynesian approach to managing the macroeconomy.

Review your own answer

Read the question below, think about it and then write your own answer. After you have done this, study the advice below and see if you can use it to improve your answer.

> **TIP**
> This question draws upon the content of Chapter 8 as well as this chapter. Longer essay questions may ask you to draw on knowledge from different sections of the syllabus.

1   Comment on the view that over many years, policies have had little or no effect on the redistribution of income and wealth and should be scrapped to allow governments to concentrate on more pressing macroeconomic problems. **[25]**

Advice on how to answer this question

- Make sure that you understand the difference between income and wealth. Make this clear in the first paragraph.

- Try not to forget about wealth in your answer. It is easier to answer for income.

- Refer to your own country and say whether policies have been effective.

- As well as benefits and the tax system, remember to include any free goods and services such as health and education.

- Think about the opportunity cost issues indicated in the wording of the question.

- Think about how effective any welfare benefits have been and whether tax revenue has been spent wisely in funding education, for example.

- Identify the main macroeconomic problems and whether more government funding might help to control them.

- Consider whether this is more beneficial than spending on redistributing income.

- Make sure your final paragraph pulls things together and that you really do answer the question.